# ENDORSEMENTS

As an adventure/adrenaline junky my entire life, I enjoyed the Go To Guy. I could relate to the stories and was encouraged in my faith as I saw them used as allegories of the Christian walk we men of faith must travel. Men have been beaten down in our culture of late, to the point where we are leery of being men, of stepping up to our responsibilities, of being the one others can count on in a bind. It's time we as men stand up in our roles as men and this book is a good start.

*Doug Englekirk*
*Zephyr Cove, NV*
*December, 2013*

"The Go To Guy challenged me in a way that all guys like to be challenged. After reading the Go To Guy I felt encouraged, equiped and ready to take on the challenge of being the Go To Guy. If you are ready for an epic journey to transform yourself into the guy that every one of us longs to be I would highly recommend checking out the Go To Guy."

*Ryan Hall*
*Olympic Marathoner*

# THE GO-TO GUY

MEN WHO ARE CAPTIVATED BY THEIR DREAMS
NOT AFRAID TO RISK IT ALL
IN THE PURSUIT OF WHAT
THE LORD HAS PLACED ON THEIR HEART

**BILLY HERMAN**

ENDORSED BY OLYMPIC RUNNER - RYAN HALL

The Go-To Guy is available at special quantity discounts for bulk purchase for sales promotions, premiums, fund-raising, and educational needs. For details write Endurance Press, 577 N Cardigan Ave Star, ID 83669.

Visit Endurance Press' website at www.endurancepress.com

The Go-To Guy
PUBLISHED BY ENDURANCE PRESS
577 N Cardigan Ave
Star, ID 83669 U.S.A.

All views expressed within are the view of the author and do not necessarily reflect the veiws of the publisher.

© Billy Herman 2014

All rights reserved. Except for brief excerpts for review purposes, no part of this book may be reproduced or used in any form without prior written permission from the publisher.

ISBN 978-0-9960146-5-6

Scriptures taken from the Holy Bible, New International Version®, NIV®. Copyright © 1973, 1978, 1984, 2011 by Biblica, Inc.™ Used by permission of Zondervan. All rights reserved worldwide. www.zondervan.com The "NIV" and "New International Version" are trademarks registered in the United States Patent and Trademark Office by Biblica, Inc.™

®2014 Billy Herman

Cover Design by Teal Rose Design Studio's

Cover and Interior Photo's courtesy Billy Herman

Printed in the United States of America

First Edition 2014

# CONTENTS

Section 1 The Approach .................. 12
    Dreaming Big ........................... 21
    Getting Real ........................... 31
    The Adventure Inside Us ................. 39
    Conditioning .......................... 51

Section 2 The Ascent ..................... 60
    Basecamp ............................. 71
    Attitude for Altitude .................... 81
    Off Route ............................. 93
    The Direct Route ...................... 103

Section 3 The Crux ...................... 114
    The Critical Moment .................... 121
    The Ledge ............................ 131
    The Crux ............................. 139
    Amidst the Trial ....................... 147

Section 4 The Descent ................... 158
    Positive Defeat ........................ 165
    Beating the Mountain .................. 177
    Living our Identity .................... 187
    The Journey Home .................... 195

# FORWARD

    Seventeen years ago in the middle of a defining and difficult time in my life, I received a card in the mail from my grandfather. I opened it and it read – *"Those who say it cannot be done, should get out of the way of the one doing it." -Chinese Proverb.*
    *Signed- Grandpa.*
    That was it. No heartfelt letter wishing me well, no money to help me out in tough times. Just a blank card with those few words printed on the front. Yet somehow that blank card was all I needed, and he knew it…
    What kind of man are you? Do you even know? Have you ever been tested? How do you measure up…? Stop. I know what you're thinking, "Enough already! Not another Christian book on manhood." We already have so many books on "Godly Manhood" and its relevant definitions with step by step guides and workbooks and seminars and retreats and teachings on how to combat the emasculation of our culture and on and on. Don't get me wrong, there are plenty of amazing Christian authors out there writing wonderful books with powerful ministries. I thank them. God bless them. This book is not trying to take away from that. However, this is not a therapeutic Gospel, or self-help book. This book isn't going to teach you to be wild and free or give you the

instruction manual to modern-day knighthood. This is just the account of one man's adventure with an honest yet challenging teaching woven throughout. This is a modern Pilgrims Progress written for the men seeking the great things God has called them to. Those men who believe he is a rewarder of those who diligently seek Him. It is Billy's heart with this story to encourage and to walk with these men who desire to be Gods men of account. His Go-To Guys.

    I've known Billy for almost fifteen years now. We have been through it: Love, sin, victory, defeat. We were the best man at each other's weddings. He is the brother I never had. We have tied miles of climbing rope between us over the years and have been on just enough epic adventures to still be here in one piece. Whether rock climbing the Sierra Nevada, ice climbing in the San Gabriels, surfing and snorkeling the Pacific, or driving across 50 miles of salt flats in Baja Mexico tracking some sketchy geo-coordinates in search of a hidden desert oasis (Long story…) we have shared some real life experiences, sharpening each other along the way. He is always challenging me to be a better friend, husband and man of God. It is almost impossible to keep up with him and he never stops. Truth is, I have always been impressed by and sometimes jealous of Billy's gifting and abilities. Not just physical but spiritual as well. He was a professional runner when we first met. He was training with the U.S. team preparing for races all around the world. He was splitting his time between altitude training in the mountains and down at the Olympic training center in San Diego. All the while leading worship at our church on Sunday. After that he joined the Navy, ran for them competitively while working as a corpsman in the operating room at the Navy hospital, helping to put our brave veterans back together. A few years later he gave up a great career and newly remodeled home to follow Gods call for his family to help lead a medical mission in Africa for the better part of a year. Who knows what else God has planned for him! Billy is a leader, in worship, in his family, at work and in the kingdom. Billy is also a dreamer. He is a visionary and a man of action. He is one of God's Go-To guys. That is what he is trying to share.

You may never run a sub-four minute mile, spend time training with Olympians and Navy Seals, or ever deal with life and death in an operating room, still, the message is the same. He shares from real life experience and the anecdotes of other men who are wholly pursuing the Lord. He is a man who knows who he is in the Lord and one who knows the Father's voice. That is how he has effect. He is a man of passion and great faith, a David in today's times of passivity and doubt.

In this book Billy shares an allegorical tale from one of our many adventures to try to light a spark in the hearts of those men who hear Gods call but are confused as to what the response should look like. There are places in this book and story where he challenges you to literally stop reading and to think, pray, or take action. These brief pauses are the first but critical steps to answering that call. It is not about imitating a guideline or following a color–by–number walk of faith. It is what you do when you close the book and walk away that matters. There are a lot of books out there that are exciting, sensational and appeal to many of men's insecurities. Unfortunately, pretending to be William Wallace, or your favorite TV character doesn't help you to be the man God has called YOU to be. These emotional pep rallies won't change your character. These are superficial bandages to spiritual wounds. Enough talk. Enough pretending. Time to do something.

…So you see, the message my grandfather was sending wasn't the proverb that was written on the front of that card, it was the blank page inside that was to speak to me. It was the unwritten message inside that lit the fire. Words were useless in times like these. Only action had a voice. He was calling me out. Out from the fear of the challenges ahead, into the fray. Out from the passivity that poisons most men into the passion of the valiant. I still have that card. It is a fond memory of that first real look in the mirror. The beginning of true accountability in my life. To not be the one on the sidelines in the last seconds, but the one who is standing in the middle of the arena when it is all on the line. The Go-To Guy.

*Joseph Donovan 12/4/13*

# A NOTE FROM THE AUTHOR

Regardless of where you stand on your beliefs of God, whether you are an old Christian, an atheist, or just not sure what you believe; it is my opinion that you have this book in your hands for a reason. Whether you were given the book, just picked it up, or were told about it, I believe you were destined at this point in your life to hear and read this book. It's my prayer that it will be an encouragement and an inspiration in your journey. Rather than blast through the book and add it to your tick list, take the time you need to process and reflect. It's after you read this book that matters.

What you will find here in these pages is the honest truth from my own life and my own struggles and triumphs along the adventure. There have been many men I have watched and trusted over the years. These men have contributed to this project by sharing their thoughts on the Go-To guy and the impact it has had on their lives at the end of each chapter.

I'm grateful for those of you who have invested and gone out on a limb to make this book a reality. Your investment into the lives of men is invaluable. Most importantly I would like to thank my amazing wife who believes in me and inspires me with her wisdom and insight. Thank you for standing with me through it all and trekking on this adventure!

*Billy*

## 2010 EVOLUTION TRAVERSE

**THE GO-TO GUY**

# LAMARCK COL
### 37.1905° N.   118.6673° W

## SECTION ONE
# THE APPROACH

As I sit and think about my dreams, I am captivated by a trip that I took with my best friend, Joe, into the heart of the Sierra's in 2010. We had always dreamt of that perfect climb, or talked about the perfect pitch to rope up on. We always planned, even though our wives laughed at us I'm sure, but we always gravitated toward that epic adventure, the adventure everything in our beings aspired to and drew us toward. This was such a trip.

# INTRODUCTION TO SECTION 1

I always imagine myself sitting on the porch with my best friend when we are in our nineties, in our rockers, shotguns in hand, waiting for the next salesman or adventure to come by; much like the movie Secondhand Lions. My dreams have been deep since I was a kid: Climb Everest, go to the Olympics as a professional athlete, win this race, climb the most difficult climb of your life, be a Navy Seal, shoot big elk in Idaho, start a restaurant, or own a vineyard. Much has been accomplished thus far, but that deep desire within to press further and harder, to go somewhere no one else has, or do something nobody has ever done; to be that person, be that guy, the one that everyone is attracted to; the one we all gravitate toward, the guy who seems to have the right decision for the right time, is still deep within me. To be the one called for support, the guy to experience an adventure with; the guy who answers the phone and reaches out a hand. I want to sit on that porch and share stories all day. I want to laugh at the ridiculous moments and contemplate the heartbreaking ones. I want to sit and be content that I accomplished my dreams, and went every place that God led and showed me in this amazing place we call the world. This book encompasses my passion to learn who that guy is. Who is the Go-To Guy? What does he look like?

As I sit and think about my dreams, I am captivated by a trip that I took with my best friend, Joe, into the heart of the Sierra's in 2010. We had always dreamt of that perfect climb, or talked about the perfect pitch to rope up on. We always planned, even though our wives laughed at us I'm sure, but we always gravitated toward that epic adventure, the adventure everything in our beings aspired to and drew us toward. This was such a trip. During conversation in my garage, Joe and I were discussing dreams and getting each other excited about certain adventures. Then Joe mentioned that one of his big dreams would be to accomplish Evolution Traverse in the Sierra's. We were both excited. We should do it! We had already committed to it in our minds. What ensued after that conversation was nothing short of a can-do attitude mixed with the desire above all else to accomplish our goal.

To understand our relationship, Joe and I are two guys driven to beat each other, no matter what we have to do, regardless of the situation. Ever since we met, we have joked our way through some epic trips and adventures, always trying to out do each other, but willing to succumb to the victor when appropriate. Joe is everything I see in a Go-To Guy. He is the perfect example of a man who can stand in a snowstorm at 13,000Ft on a cliff and laugh at adversity. He is the guy I can pray through serious trouble with. He is the friend on the other line willing to do anything to help a friend in need. He is gentle, a man that has a deep connection to his wife, one that would do anything to protect his family and relationship with Christ. He struggles in his life walk, just like all of us; however, he has that special ability to rise above to the next level. To push through, never give up, fight the fight, and give everything to finish strong.

Our trip unfolded as we researched good times to do the climb and plan the trip. We were in this funny time of life where both of us were determined to find the lightest, warmest, high altitude climbing equipment that can either be super expensive or downright funny depending on how far you get into it. Meaning, you can buy a 12 oz waterproof jacket that is tested in space, but it will cost you $500 bucks. Or, you can add duct tape to a plastic water bottle, minimizing your weight, and costing about $1 dollar. Whatever your approach, Joe would always call me and make comments about how his pack was going to be lighter because of this or that. Most of his comments ended with the jab that he would probably have to carry me out as well. Oh man. It got crazy.

I would call Joe one day to brag: "I just did 5,000 vertical feet of running/walking up and down this crazy trail over rocks with a 60 pound pack".

He would call a few days later and respond: "I just finished this 5 hour epic mountain bike ride on my single speed mountain bike!"

Single speed? Really?

It got ugly! None-the-less, we were both in great shape as we approached the late July date for Evolution Traverse (ET). We even built a climbing wall on the side of my house that went up to the second story. We put compression bolts right into the thick stucco and called it good. We didn't have money for the good holds, so we built wood holds and suffered through those until we could get smaller, better holds. Joe kept telling me the holds were too big or how much of a wuss I was. To set the record straight, Joe and I are not newcomers to the climbing world. Both of us come from hardcore climbing backgrounds and although our bodies are not as rigid as they once were (although Joe would say his is) we know the ridge was doable for us. Regardless, we had done the research and were determined to put this climb into the books.

Evolution is a J-shaped, 8-mile, 9-summit ridge traverse; cherished for its pristine granite and regarded by most in the Sierra's as the hardest and most rewarding ridge traverse. It requires relentless sections of free climbing on a knife-edge ridge at 5.9 VI between 12,500 feet to 13,835 feet on high quality alpine granite with 10,000 feet of elevation gain and loss during the traverse. Peter Croft holds the unbelievable record with a 15-hour one-day solo record. By no means did we think we were going to do this traverse in 15 hours, but we were willing to spend the night on Mount Darwin and use it as a bivy for a two-day epic climbing adventure. This was our plan.

One of the big setbacks to ET is there is limited water supply to start with. Depending on the time of the year there might not be any at all, unless you downclimb to a lake, boil snow water, or find runoff during the traverse. The longer you take on a climb, the more gear you have to bring. Having both lived at altitude in Mammoth Lakes, CA before, we knew that driving up from San Diego, we were both going to have to be very smart about our acclimatization and ascent onto the traverse. Our stocking list was the usual assortment of gear we knew we needed; from certain aid protection to a good light dynamic rope that would help us through some of the more technical sections. Since we were going to sleep on the ridge we needed to bring a stove for food and melting snow for water. We calculated every detail. We watched the weather in the weeks leading up to the trip. Everything was coming together nicely. We were both training and prepared as best we could, considering we were living at sea level. As anyone who has spent time in the Sierra's knows, the weather can never be fully forecasted or predicted. As our adventure began to unfold, nothing was closer to the truth.

## ONE
# Dreaming Big

I am a big dreamer. No doubt about it. Growing up I could conjure up vast wars between GI Joe men and bases, and somehow combine my space-legos into the fight. I would create huge battles that lasted for weeks between these plastic warriors. As I got older, the battles moved outside where I would have my backpack with the essentials and my weapons of choice (usually pipes and wood weapons made in the garage). Then there would be a huge battle leading up to barrel rolls through the yard and bushes, back into the trees, and then somewhere in the battle would be my mom, screaming at me to get back in the house for dinner. Whatever the dreams, I was always having them. As I got older my dreams shifted into outdoor adventures involving climbing and soccer, running and hunting. As I started to get into running in high school and won a few state cross country championships, I started to dream big, towards goals of colleges to go to and even making an Olympic team. We were created to dream.

Where do these dreams come from? Where do we get these vast visions that seem to be impossible? It seems, as I have gotten older, I have learned to push my dreams aside, belittling them, only to come up with some selfish form of the right path to take. A path that inevitably removes me from any path that God ever had for me. I can think back to so many decisions in life that I had a chance to dream big but conjured my way out of it somehow. Are we scared? What keeps us from diving into those sacred crazy dreams deep in our hearts?

    I'm writing this book to pursue what it means to be the Go-To Guy; the guy that keeps dreaming. The one who is not afraid to go after the impossible because he knows it is possible. I want to be real with you. I am not a writer. I am not a speaker or somebody of importance, a pastor or biblical scholar. What I am is a man that wants to pursue the heart of God at all costs. What I am is a man that believes in my own dreams enough to push aside any preconceived notion of men today and what the world thinks we can accomplish. I am a man of integrity and energy, full of dreams in my heart. I believe in myself, and what God can do through me. Most importantly, I believe the Holy Spirit wants to teach us men what it means to be Go-To Guys and the importance of laying it all at His feet to pursue the dreams He first had for us. I am a dreamer. I have big things in my heart. Take a second and think about some crazy dreams in your heart. Maybe the ones you haven't told your wife, or the dream you think couldn't possibly happen until you finish school. Maybe your dream is the culmination of many small dreams. Whatever it is, take a second to think about that dream.

What is stopping us from dreaming big? Why are we managing our dreams so that we can somehow quantify why we never got there? Think about your dream, and take a second to ask the Holy Spirit to come in and show you what He has for you in your dream. Don't laugh. Actually, stop reading this and ask the Holy Spirit to show you what He has for you in this dream of yours (say your dream to the Lord).

Whatever pops up in your head after you prayed that, I want you to write down in the front cover of this book. You see, sometimes we are afraid to actually ask God for the things He has already promised us as men. The purpose of this is to listen to what the Holy Spirit is saying about your dream. Not what we think of the dream, but what the Holy Spirit thinks. In doing this, we are inviting the Lord into your dream. We are laying at His feet the dream we have and asking Him what He thinks. He already knows our dreams. I can't think of anybody greater than our Papa, our Daddy, our Father, who wants to give us the desires of our hearts. As most of you dads know, you would be hard pressed to find a dad or father out there that doesn't want to give his kids their desires. Every father wants his kids to dream. Dream big. Our Heavenly Father wants us to dream huge; to dream the impossible. When we give that dream back, it enters us into the relationship He desires with us and enables us to hear what He has to say. Many dreams I have tried to attain through myself have flopped, only to have the Lord give it back to me when I have submitted myself to Him and given Him my dream. We cannot, as men, fully attain our dreams without letting go of all our pride and selfishness. I squandered what little professional running career I had after college because I failed to fully give God my dreams. Making the Olympic team was achievable, but in my own strength, fighting my own way through, I was unable to make that team. When I learned to surrender and give up my dream, it was amazing to watch God open doors to fulfilling that dream in my heart.

So why all the talk about dreams you say? Do you have some unfulfilled dreams in your heart? Dreaming big enables us to take a risk, invite the adventure. It builds purpose. All of these characteristics are found in the Go-To Guy. In my small opinion I think the world has done a great job of eliminating risk from our daily lives. Risk has all but been eliminated from the daily grind. We have been deceived that risk invites trouble. We're told it encourages problems to arise, and dreams to disappear. In fact, risk does the opposite. It invites us to push into our dreams and take a chance. A better way of saying it; it actually forces us to have faith in what was thought impossible. Through faith, He makes all things possible. He is the perfector of our faith. Our challenge as men with dreams is to have the faith to take the risk. To step out in boldness and believe that this dream in our heart, the dream placed there by our Heavenly Father is possible. This belief rests at the core of the Go-To Guy.

I'd be crazy to sit here and say risk always brings success. Risk can also look like failure as well. Meaning, many men take risks but fail in their endeavors. Thomas Edison failed too many times to count, but each failure was a success and an invention of something else. It may not have been the end goal that Edison was after, but his ability to continue to push forward in risk and take chances led to the many inventions that we all live with today. He holds an incredible 1,093 patents. In some of those patents were some failures, but his resolve to continually see a problem and want to make it faster and more productive, invited the dreams and risk to keep going after what he thought could be better.

> "Our greatest weakness lies in giving up. The most certain way to succeed is always to try just one more time. I have not failed. I've just found 10,000 ways that won't work." Thomas A. Edison (brainyquotes.com)

We all will fail at something in our lives, but if we change our mindset to see stepping out in our dreams as a positive thing, regardless of whether we win or fail, we will be successful just like Edison was. If we step out and go after something only to fail, we must, as men, believe in the dreams in our hearts and continue on. I believe that as we focus our minds on going after the risk, it will open us up to actually being able to fail and see that as positive.

One of the hardest things for me in my life has been stepping forward in the risk. Most who know me would say risk is easy for me. In some cases, risk is easy. I have no problem taking a huge fall on a big climb in Yosemite, or jumping out of a perfectly good airplane, but when my job is on the line, bills need to be paid, the remodel needs to be funded, and the commute just seems to be getting longer, how do we take a risk on some dream that has slowly melted away? As men we have calculated out the risk and cost of failure. We want to leave a legacy. We desire to provide for our family. We want to be valuable and have our work matter. We want to be successful. Have an impact. But we find safety in mediocrity because it requires no risk.

One of my best friends stated to me, "Why did it take sixteen years for me to get comfortable with taking a risk with my dream?" It lies in the comfort. We dwell on the fear of the risk instead of the promise we have in Jesus. The fear says, "we will lose our house, we will lose our job." It may say, "my wife will leave me, my kids won't trust me, I won't be of any worth." Then we as men start to internalize and take it personal. We bury our dreams because we do not want them to hurt us or take away the things we have worked hard for. We look to weekend hunting trips and vacations to provide us our short dose of adrenaline, a small taste of risk without any consequences. I propose this. What if we uncovered our dreams? What if we told our wives and our kids, our friends and family our dreams? What if we as men dropped to our knees and laid that knapsack full of the biggest dreams we have at the feet of Jesus? I believe the Go-To Guy is willing to go there. I waited years to take my step. It took all I had, but I was willing to lay down the great job, the house by the beach, the career, and our awesome church, because of one simple truth: I knew in my heart I was not walking out the dreams God had for me. Ouch. Are you walking out the dreams in your heart? Last year, I quit my job, rented out my house for two years, and embarked on a 6-month trip to Africa with my wife to pursue what God had for me . Through the trip I was able to hear God, listen to God, and learn to not be afraid of what He has for our dreams. I'm here to tell you the grass isn't any greener, but the risk and the step forward invited more than I could ever imagine. I was able to once again invite the adventure. I thought it was gone. For a kid from Idaho, losing the adventure can kill you in your heart. The mountains are everything to me. I grew up watching my dad cast flies onto glistening rivers, watching trout roll up to a fly, seeing the beauty in the simple cast of a fly rod; the quiet perfectness of it all. I thought that was gone. That one step, whether large or small into the risk, invites the adventure.

Much like parents are thrilled at their son's first steps, or their daughter's piano recital, our Heavenly Father is dying to jump for joy when we take the steps necessary to fulfill our purpose. That purpose comes directly from the risk that invites the adventure. I have seen first hand in my own life how I have complained about the lack of adventure and purpose in my life. My wife would probably say I have complained a lot. Ironically I was complaining about the very things I was unwilling or not stepping into. Instead of dreaming big, taking a risk, and pursuing the adventure, I would dream big and complain about all the ways that I wasn't able to get there. I was using excuses to let the dreaming happen but fearful of the risk it would take to live alive and pursue my heart. My question here is, "Are you dreaming big?" Much like Joe and I on Evolution Traverse, we were dreaming big, taking a risk, living our dream with purpose. The Go-To Guy is not afraid to step into his dreams. We accomplish this by allowing the Lord to have our dreams. By laying down our deepest longings and desires, knowing He gives them, we give back control of those dreams so He can work out the purpose He has for us. When we become free of our control, we live in freedom to pursue those dreams with no fear and reckless abandon.

I'll be the first to admit that not one person on this planet could have stopped Joe and I from going into the mountains that summer to go after that dream.

The heart of the Go-To Guy is deep and dreaming big represents a huge part of God's call and vision for our life. As we step into being Go-To Guys, we have to be resolute in our pursuit to believe in our dreams and actively walk them out with faith, perseverance, and purpose.

## GO-TO GUY Response

*There are several other instances and adventures I have been on with friends that have pushed me outside my comfort zone, which in the long run helped me get over my fears and trust God more. They (Go-To Guys) have had a profound impact in my life. These guys have redirected the course of my life more than once. I still remember a quote from my good friend, Brian. He said, "I wish I would have taken more risks when I was younger." The context was following God and stepping out more in faith and trust in Him. I think about this statement often, which pushes me beyond my comfort zone in following God and His will for my life.*

*-Tyler*

## TWO
# Getting Real

I was thinking back to when I was in high school. I was part of the drama team at my church. We had a very eclectic group of young men and women, and one very gifted teacher. We were presented and taught a mime that told a story through these faces that we all wore up on stage as masks. It was set to music and extremely powerful. What was impactful about the mime was that each character had these white plastic masks with different faces on them that we all wore. It wasn't until the story was revealed to the audience that each character started to show and reveal their true face underneath the mask. I wonder if we as men chose to show our one true face, instead of the closet full of masks that we wear in each situation, what it would be like? You know what I'm talking about. Your wife, or family, best friend, roommate or sibling, is really the only one who truly knows the real you; the authentic you. Why then do we roam around wearing other masks that do not truly represent who we are?

How many faces do you have? Seriously? How many faces do you have? Do you ever put on a different mask when you walk into a situation that requires one of you? The Go-To Guy has one face. He was only born with one face: his one true authentic face. It is made up with distinct features that only you have. So lets get real here. How many masks do you have? Here's what I mean. When you go on a date, you dress your best and spend two days before thinking out every scenario for the perfect time. You get the flowers. We make ourselves out to be the best we can. We try and impress in every way we can. We don't show our weaknesses. We only want to show our good stuff. That's a mask. I'm not condoning going on a date and unloading all your junk to some poor woman! I'm using it as an example of how we put on masks that do not accurately represent who we are. You can be authentic with the real you. I'm sure most women would appreciate going on a date with a man that is confident enough to avoid hiding behind a mask.

We have our work mask. You know, the one that says yes to everything your boss throws at you. The one who has trouble standing up for something he knows is wrong; the mask that clearly is just looking for advancement or the next promotion. One of my closest friends repeatedly kept denying promotions from his workplace because he stayed true to what he loved to do and what he felt God calling him to do. In the end, the Lord has blessed this Go-To Guy because of his faithfulness to stay true to his calling and destiny.

My favorite is the church mask. You know, where the guy is all about going to church and smiling, saying all the right Biblical things, then living out something entirely different when he leaves the building. These plastic faces are developed from years of coping and survival. They come from years of getting torn down. They come from a lack of confidence in identity. Each mask is a direct reflection of our own insecurities.

Why are we not willing to just have one face for every situation? I get frustrated that many Christian men tend to show something they are not, in order to not show who they really are. Why are we afraid to show the real us? The devil does a great job at keeping us from diving deep into who we are in our identity. He keeps us uncomfortable and insecure with our self worth, which in turn keeps us comfy with our many masks. Much like dreaming, the devil keeps us alternating out our many masks. The true authentic guy keeps his one face because he knows it is what was given him and he is sure of it. The best part is it is not a mask. It is you! Do you ever wonder how that one random guy you know always has the right answer to your deepest questions? The Go-To Guy answers from his heart, not his mask. He answers from the real-time friend that he is. He is willing to show weakness because he knows it encourages growth and from growth comes maturity. His confidence is in Christ not his mask. He knows that if he lives from within and through his relationship and identity in Christ, he shows his real face with nothing to hide. As we trust the authenticity given us, we can walk in confidence that each step is going to appear for us to walk on in our journey.

Generically looking at the movie Indian Jones and the Last Crusade, we see Indy run through a cave only to end at a huge chasm. Indy has to make a decision to trust in faith that the empty deep chasm in front of him has a bridge that cannot be seen. By faith he takes the risk of stepping into the abyss only to have his foot solidly land on the first invisible step. After his first step he realizes he must walk by faith; that each step will appear as he moves forward.

Being authentic requires of us the faith to take that step; to be real. The Go-To Guy only has one face. It is real and authentic, not a mask. It means that we stand tall in the midst of hard or troubling times. We are never given more than we can handle. In fact, the Lord prepares us with our life circumstances for what's coming next. As men we have to be comfortable with who we are. We have to be confident in what God has placed in our hearts. I'm getting at the fact that we have many masks and after a few years those masks start to become who we are instead of the one authentic face God intends for us to show the world. The Go-To Guy is far from perfect, but he is real. The Go-To Guy will give it to you straight up. It won't be sugar coated. It might sting. What it will be though is authentic and as real as it comes. I recently had some tough issues going on and I happened to be kayaking on Shasta Lake in Redding, Ca. I called Joe from that lake and asked him for some real advice. What I have come to expect is not the answer but someone who is willing to walk me through the decision process and in love keep me tracking in the right direction. That is the authentic Go-To Guy. The one who cares enough to dive into your crap, without knowing anything about it, and help you walk it out. Being authentic keeps us real. It keeps us in the true direction God has for our life. As we dream, we welcome the adventure, as we get authentic, we are learning to ditch the masks we wear and be the men we were created for in every situation.

We can't live out the dreams God has given us without being authentic. Watching some Go-To Guys I look up to, I have recognized that authenticity comes in the form of transparency. It is what I love most about my best friend. I can guarantee that every time we talk it is real and what you see is really what you get.

> *"Authentic Christians are transparent. What you see is what you get with them. They have learned through hard experiences that the transparent life is more likely to bring them the joy and peace of the Kingdom, so they are honest about what is happening in their own lives and they are honest about issues they have with other people.*

> *Transparent people learn the wisdom of living according to John's plea that we be transparent in our relationship with God, with ourselves, and with other people (see 1 John 1:7-9). That is, we live in confession of our sins, we find forgiveness of our sins, and we walk in truth and light with God and with others."*
> -Dr. Richard d. Dobbins

Walking in the light gives us freedom to be and grow. We recognize the need for intimacy with the Father, and from the overflow of the heart wisdom comes. Why is it that authentic men are sought after? They represent a truth that cannot be overlooked. They are trusted. Christian or not, many business owners will surround themselves with upright and trustworthy people. They recognize the valuable. The Go-To Guy recognizes the value in which he is in Christ and walks in confidence knowing that his wisdom and realness comes from the experiences that he encounters in adventures. We must be transparent, willing to throw away any masks we have created. We must be willing to throw them all down so we can truly come alive in who we are.

> *"The need for authenticity should never be greater than the value for love. Learn how to serve the church with love, patience, and humility. Commit your life and your gifts for the long haul!!"* -Brian Johnson tweet

This is it guys. It took me years to even realize I had a closet full of different masks. Each thing in life that brought me down seemed to get a new mask. As I have gone through and started taking authority over each area I have made a mask for, I am free to live out who I really am. Think of it this way. Your whole face is covered in a thick layer of dry cracked red clay. It hasn't seen life and growth in years. Some years it rains but most of the time it stays cracked. Nothing can grow, and if it does it withers and dies soon. Gently the Lord begins to remove a piece of clay, one by one, until light starts to break through the cracks. Eventually your whole face begins to be revealed in one bright likeness of Christ in you. You shine brightly and bring light to dark places. This is how the Go-To Guy lives out authenticity. By living from his identity, he is able to rid himself of the mask and walk around as a light. We are drawn toward the light. This is why we seek after or long for Go-To Guys in our lives. We need the wisdom and encouragement; we in turn can live out the Go-To Guy in each of us. I challenge you to commit to laying down your masks for the sake of it all, and live from the face you have. The face you are. Christ in you.

### GO-TO GUY Response

*In a single word: AUTHENTICITY. Outside of Jesus, perfection isn't going to be found in a "Go-To Guy", so the next best thing is honest and humble authenticity. I find myself wanting to follow men who exhibit this trait far more than I want to follow those with a "clean" exterior. When I get real about myself I need to know that the "Go-To Guy" I am getting real with is also real about himself. I have come across several authentic "Go-To Guys" in the course of my life and while each has their blinds spots, they are willing to "go there" and not afraid of showing their human side. Sadly, I have also come across many "upstanding Christian men" who are unwilling to "go there" and that's irritating, sad and frustrating. Especially since that is much more common.*

*-Bill*

## THREE
# The Adventure Inside Us

*"Someone once said, "The problem with life is that it is so daily." I agree! Many of us have great ideas about life, about what it should be like and how we can become successful at it. But for most of us, the struggle lies in daily walking out our convictions - especially when it comes to thinking in such a way that our minds don't violate our hearts. Ultimately, true success lies in your ability to manage your inner life, the secret kingdom that lives within you. It is really impossible to control your behavior long-term unless you master your thoughts and subject them to the virtues that you have chosen to live by.....Your virtues train your attitudes, attitudes dictate your choices, choices decide your behavior, and your behavior determines your destiny" -Kris Vallotton Purity Book Chapter 4, pg 86-87*

My whole life encompasses adventure. It's wrapped in my thoughts, my dreams, and my goals. It's hard not to be adventurous when we dream big. It's no wonder that when I get tied down at work, or bogged down in a project, it limits my dreaming and the adventure starts to slip away into the fray. My biggest struggle right now is with my identity. I will have amazing moments and worship with God where I feel filled up and unstoppable in my quest for adventure in my heart, then it seems a discouraging event will happen and I resort back to the life of status quo. "Status quo" could be an addiction you struggle with, staring for hours at porn, or conflicts with loved ones. What causes us to steer from our identity? Recently I have struggled with porn. It is a battle my wife and I have won. The reason I bring this up is that we cannot live out our identity when we are blocking it with sin and lies. Living a hidden lie like porn was destroying everything I had in a God-given identity. As we step away from our true identity and start believing a false identity that the devil clearly wants for us, we make agreements with that identity and start walking it out. Porn was an avenue to cover up deeper issues that I failed to communicate and keep in the light with my wife. This is why we must remain in our true identity from God. As we walk in our virtues that guide our ultimate destiny we can weather the storms that come (porn in my case) and walk in freedom, which is the real us. Enter the Go-To Guy into the world!

The life of young David in the Bible, an eventual King, is a great example of walking out your virtues.

David spent his whole childhood protecting sheep, tending flocks, protecting, honoring, and learning his identity. As the Lord showed him, and David embraced his identity, it prepared him for the ultimate showdown with Goliath, the Philistine. He walked right up and out of his identity, and rose to the destiny God had for his life. He slung that rock and dropped the giant! Imagine if David had never spent any time growing and tending to the sheep in the wilderness. What if he grew up stealing and going to brothels, living an untrustworthy life? I would venture to say the outcome of that day on the battlefield would have been much different, and may not have even happened. God has our days predestined. He knows our mistakes and triumphs. We have a choice of whether to live out the Go-To Guy in all of us, or we can venture off on our own. How could we ever out- imagine God? How could we ever think that we could have a better plan for our lives than God Himself? As the classic Go-To Guy David from the Bible shows us, we must live in our identity so that we can bring heaven to earth and show God's will and destiny for each of our lives.

    Identity is the foundation for all that comes next. It dictates our next move and clearly allows us to commune with our Savior at the deepest level. Listen to me carefully when I say this. Your identity is the core and deepest place of your relationship in Christ. It allows us to live out the destiny and sacred romance the Father has for us. It makes us into the

Go-To Guy. If you take nothing else from this book, take this, that we must know our identity in Christ and live out that identity to our destiny. Pause. Take a moment. Stare at a wall. Whatever…but reflect for a second and ask yourself what is my identity?

Your life may never be the same as we ask Holy Spirit to show us what our identity is. Take a moment, block out all distractions, and say the words, "Holy spirit, what is my identity?" In your moment, listen to what He says to you. Whatever pops in your head, write it down. If you are sincere in your question, God will be serious and real in His response to your question. As my wife has said: "Identity is not what you do, it's who you are….men are motivated to do, and you need to know who you are, to do what you are supposed to". That's a good word!

You may now be thinking, great Billy, but what the heck are my virtues and my identity? Good question. As you ponder this, realize we are in this together. Meaning the Go-To Guy values his relationships with other men because there is value in what they can read into in our own lives. As we come to a deeper relationship with other men, we can develop ways to encourage each other and not be afraid to ask the real questions, or get to the root of the issues. If you lack close guy relationships in your life, ask the Lord to bring you some. These men will be some of your biggest assets besides your wife if you are married.

I'm always amazed when I look up a certain word in the dictionary. The definition of "identity" is: 1. sameness of essential or generic character in different instances, 2. The distinguishing character or personality of an individual (2012 Merriam Webster inc)." As I started to look at my own identity (many years and sleepless nights), a few questions came up. What is my identity? What are the essential qualities and virtues that are core to who I am? I love how the definition says, "in different instances". This means your character and all that it is made of is the same in all circumstances. Your identity is the same in all your circumstances. Like we talked about being authentic, you are not authentic in one situation and then put on a different mask, to represent something different in another instance. That wouldn't be authentic. Your identity is the same across the board. As we recognize what "they" are, we can live out our character, your distinguishing personality in all that you do. This is the core of the Go-To Guy. You are unwavering in your circumstances because you know that God made you this way and your life and destiny is purposed by your ability to know who you are!! It's important to say this as well. We are all different in our characters and make-up. Being a Go-To Guy means you are true to your identity and personality. There is no exact mold of the perfect Go-To Guy. You walk it out and live it. The world deserves it! God designed it.

My personal motto is, 'Living the dream'. Why do I always say that to people? Because I am living out the identity and purpose in my life! It might not be perfect, but I'm on a huge adventure! Whether I'm rockin out to techno while plowing our dirt road on a tractor, at a remote cabin in the woods, hunting for big game in the wilderness, climbing the route of my life, or going after the deep-seated dreams for a new business or career; I'm going after what God has placed in my heart. This is a huge struggle for men. If you are at a place where you are saying: "What am I doing?" I would focus on your identity. Particularly looking closely at who you are.

So who are you? What makes you tick? What are you dreaming big about and desire most to do? Deep in the heart of Idaho, is a remote place where the Lord has and continues to show up for me. It is in this place where I have asked the Lord to show me who I am and what my purpose is. I awoke one night at this place, as it seems God has chosen between 2-4am to speak to me consistently. I noticed the glow of the fireplace in the small dark shadowy room. In that dead silent place, the Lord began to download audibly to me my name and the meaning. What He spoke to me was a confirmation and an affirmation of who I am. His word brought meaning to confusion in my own life and clarity to what lay ahead. What is important here is that I finally positioned my heart to hear what God was saying to me. I'm sure He had been saying it for years I just wasn't listening. I was too busy complaining that I couldn't hear from God. As men on this journey, I am sharing this with you to encourage you to find your place where God speaks. When you find it, hang there. Spend time there. Cultivate a lifestyle that allows you to get fed. I'm not condoning less church, or more Bible studies, or less connection with wife or girlfriend. Time is hard to eek out of this busy life. Just cherish and give value to the one thing that fills you up and keeps you more alive than anything: our relationship with Papa Daddy.

Isn't it interesting that Cabelas and REI are packed with men running out of the stores with the latest hunting, fishing, or backpacking gear? Or that the NFL is some of most watched TV during the fall? For most men, coming alive entails going hunting, breathing the mountain air, killing stuff, freezing to death in a duck blind, watching Peyton Manning win the game and his 10 commercials, playing the newest Halo or Spec Ops game, or some other absurd adventure that most our loved ones roll their eyes at. Men will conjure up the craziest excuse to get something they want or desire! They will go to the ends of the earth to experience a tidbit of what they desire. Why?! Why do we not go after Christ the way we go after that new climbing jacket or fly rod? Why do we not pursue Christ like we pursued our girlfriends or wives? Maybe you do. Maybe you are the model guy. The perfect example of all that Christ has, but I doubt it. You have screwed up at least once. I'm calling you out. It's time that men rise up to seek after the one relationship that breaths life to our identity and launches us into all we are supposed to be. At the cabin I finally realized it. It was time to be a son. What are you doing to position yourself to be a son? Ponder this for a second. The prodigal son left to pursue the life and things that in the end the father gives him! As Paul Manwaring once said: "The problem isn't with the dad, the issue is with the son. If you are not a son, every father will let you down. Inheritance without identity is a bunch of cash."(Finding Father's, Bethel sermon Jan 16, 2011) Consider for a moment you being the younger son in this story. Now lets take a look at this story. There are two sons in Luke 15:11-31. The younger son asks for his inheritance and after the father concedes, the son runs off to "squander his wealth in wild living (vs 13)." After all his money runs out, a great famine hits the land and the son tends to pigs to survive. He then realizes that even his father's hired hands have leftover food when they eat, and so it's then that he realizes what he has done. This is when the redemptive process begins and the son comes home to become a son. He positions himself under the father to receive his inheritance. The father then has to correct the older son who becomes angry that the father received the younger son back, explaining that the younger son was lost and deceived, and now has righted his path. He became a son again. We have an amazing father! The younger son looks at his life and realizes that without coming under the father and receiving from Him as a son, his true identity will be kept from Him. We have to cultivate that sonship with our Heavenly Father to receive all He has for our identity and us. When we do this it allows us to see clearly and hear what He is saying about us.

> *"Position to be a son. We have to live for that. Father gives you your identity. We position our hearts to recognize what the father has to offer. Learning that our identity will always flourish under the extravagant father."* -Paul Manwaring, Finding Father's, Bethel Sermon Jan 16, 2011

I'm going to say this again. Your identity is the core and deepest place of your relationship in Christ. It allows us to live out the destiny and sacred romance the father has for us. We must know our identity in Christ and live out that identity to our destiny. Your identity distinguishes you from everyone else. Instead of wishing you were someone else why not show the world whom you are and what makes you amazing in God's eyes? What character traits are you portraying in different instances in your life? In my life, this was where I had to really seek being a son, and give the Lord my heart so I could be in a position to hear what He was saying to me. I'm not buying the statement, "the Lord is not speaking to me." If the Lord is not speaking to you, it should reflect to you the need you have to commune deeper with Him. Learn to recognize the red flags. If we align ourselves to get that inheritance as a true son, you will be blown away at the favor God has for you. The Go-To Guy lives from his identity. Isn't it about time you did too? Bill Johnson sums it up nicely...

> "So as I navigate the various challenges and obstacles on the highway to my destiny, I'm watching the warning lights of my heart. I must sustain my connection with the source of life. Really, there's only one light---the oil light. It's the oil of His presence that gives me everything I need and anoints me to fulfill my purpose. But He only gives me the measure of His presence that I'm willing to jealously guard. So I have to build the strength of will and character to focus all my energies on carrying His presence with excellence. I can't afford to have a moment in my life when the circumstances distract me from tending that fire in my heart---even a situation when I must tend the fire by myself." Bill Johnson Strengthen Yourself in the Lord pg. 48

## *GO-TO GUY Response*

In my mind the "Go-To Guy" is a father or friend in my life who I trust to go to for help, counseling, advice, coaching, encouragement, or they are just an ear to listen. The trust I have in this person is built through relationship. Most often the way the relationship was built helps grow trust in certain areas of my life with that person. When tough times come I feel comfortable "going to the guy" I have built a relationship with for the area of my life that I need help with. A characteristic of my "Go-To Guys" are trust that they can and will help in whatever area because they have my best interest in mind. It could all be summed up in love! The "Go-To Guy" always has the talent or gift that I need them to use in my life. The relationship process has built a trust in me that they will use their talent or gift in love to help me. To sum it up, the identity of my "Go-To Guy" is a gift or talent used because they have love for me, a brother.

–Justin

## FOUR
# Conditioning

I recently had the opportunity to help train and pace a close friend of mine as he prepared for the London Olympics in the marathon. Day in and day out we went after what the plan was. We would do 10-16 mile tempo runs, running a certain pace, me on the bike, Ryan running. We were determined to see this through. How do we condition ourselves for the little things as well as the big things like the Olympics? In preparing for the biggest stages of our life, how do we as men dig deep and use all that training and dedication to produce the conditioning we need for the long haul? I believe we can as men condition ourselves to be mentally and physically prepared for all that we strive to do, but it is painful and often times requires everything we have to see it through. It was fascinating to me as I watched my friend Ryan persevere through the toughest of workouts, eat only the best foods for his body, and have his entire world and schedule revolve around training. As a former athlete as well, I understand the grueling lifestyle where everything is placed on the backburner to training. It takes the utmost dedication to pursue our dreams. In this case, watching Ryan condition himself in all areas of his life for the Olympic dream. Much like the Olympic dream, operating from our hearts in life allows us to step deeper into our relationship with Him, and gain understanding of what our purpose is more clearly as we grow closer to Him. I want to look at how the Go-To Guy positions himself to be ready for the journey.

What makes special operations guys who are Navy SEALS special or different? These men graduate the toughest school in the world and pass the most grueling tests of dedication and determination. What gives them the edge they need to go farther and push harder than anyone else, accomplish that goal, finish their mission? Some obvious traits come to mind. Endurance, strength, mental toughness, and the ability to focus are a few. While I believe these are physical and mental attributes to have in our conditioning, we also need to look at the heart and what it means to condition ourselves for the long haul; life. How do we condition ourselves to finish strong? Strong past the gold medal at the Olympics, past the next drop behind enemy lines, past the phone call we get about our wife having cancer, past the stress of losing our jobs; how do we condition ourselves to stay positive, love from our depths, and rise to our destiny? Preparing for the approach is about dreaming big, being authentic, our identities, but most of all conditioning ourselves to be operators on a mission, ready to be deployed anywhere, anytime. To be conditioned for living out our dreams and identities, authentic to the core.

Conditioning is the culmination of our dreams, our identities, and authenticity, making us who we are in our approach and lifelong destiny. When we stay true to ourselves and live from our identities and dreams, we walk out God's destiny and plan for us. We live life from the core of our being. The direct result is that we stay focused on our God given abilities and flourish in those.

As a former Corpsman in the Navy, I can tell you from experience, there are many who aspire to be a SEAL, but fail out at some point between A schools, SCRUFT duty, Indoc, or at BUD/S when they ring out. They may be med boarded (medical injury) or just can't continue on. I found that most who bailed out were men who did not prepare or did not know what they were getting into mentally or physically. The men, who make it through, were men who at their core were walking out what they are, not pretending or wanting to be somebody else. I am sure there is a correlation between Navy SEAL ads on TV and recruitment. You never see a TV ad for working in the galley on a submarine for 6 months underwater! Men want at their core to be a SEAL, the best of the best. We can't join the Navy to be a SEAL only because we want what they have. At your core you have to believe and know that being a SEAL is at the core of who you are.

If you are an engineer, the last place we need you is high point covering your platoon as they raid a compound in the mountains of Afghanistan. We need you building the bridge or dam project of your dreams. You get my point? The secrecy, honor, integrity of SEALS is appealing but as we condition ourselves as Go-To Guys, we live from our core and walk out those same qualities in everything we do regardless of what we do.

How do we condition as Go-To Guys ? This is a lifelong pursuit. Not a new year's resolution. This is a commitment, the long haul. This is the marathon, not the 100m. We don't walk to the altar with the woman of our dreams to give her a week's worth of our love and attention. We walk hand in hand in a covenant, promising to love and protect her till we die. Some men have a hard time with commitment, and struggle with the long haul. I would venture to say they are struggling with deeper issues and as we leave the agreements we've made with sin to walk in our true identities, we align ourselves with the fullness of God's will for us. This is how we condition ourselves. We dedicate our whole beings to the identities we carry. We train in the ways that keep us positioned and aligned with our relationship in Christ.

I mentioned I struggled with porn earlier in the book. I had to learn that porn was meeting a need I had deeply buried inside, that my wife could not meet my needs. I had to condition myself to first be free of every secret and lie in my life. This meant coming out with the truth to my wife. Detailing to her my struggle. As I did this I was coming under the freedom in Christ as a forgiven son; learning and conditioning myself to recognize what had caused me to get trapped by porn. As I trained myself to see these areas, I conditioned myself to walk in authority over them. We have the will power to say no by our authority in Christ. We keep sin in the light, instead of the darkness. I'm telling you, it has nowhere to go. I dedicated myself to seeking after keeping the light in my marriage. When I screw up it breaks my heart when I have to tell my wife. It only took me two times to realize I was tired of putting her through the ringer. She had to understand my battle as well. As we have fought it and won, we now have in place ways to combat the onslaught pointed at men. Most importantly, though, I have trained myself to be on the offense when it comes to protecting and training myself to stay free of porn. This is the core of the Go-To Guy. We cannot, as men, sin, get forgiveness, but still live in the agreement and sin again. We will always make mistakes but what I mean is this: we get stuck in this trap because the root issues never get brought to light. Prepare yourself for the battle of your life!

There is not a forward deployed Navy SEAL anywhere in the world that has not prepared over and over for the mission at hand. There is not an Olympic athlete that just shows up at the Olympic Games without first preparing physically and mentally for that moment when everything comes together. I feel this is your moment to come to grips with your struggles, to fight the fight, to win the battle that keeps you down. This is the moment to condition yourself for the climb of your life! What I'm suggesting here is that you seriously stop reading and reflect for a second about conditioning yourself. I'm dead serious when I say this is the time to make a change. Your conditioning directly reflects all that God has for you and your life. I'm suggesting that we all live from our God given identities and destinies. I feel God calling us men to make a change; a change that requires us to take a step. For some of you this may be a painful step. This book is not a self help book or how-many-steps-does-it-take-to-get-something-book. This book is about getting real with ourselves. As we pursue what it means to be a Go-To Guy, we have to position our hearts to listen and hear clearly from the Lord. We can't live from our hearts without first being free of all that traps us, all that holds us down.

Do you ever have that moment when you feel it rising inside you? You have the perfect song going. You might be driving. You might be riding a high at work. You may be watching your kids win a big race or game. That place where you feel invincible. You may have just seen the woman of your dreams. Sometimes words cannot express best the feelings and emotions we have. Music speaks deeply to me.

As a worship leader, my heart screams to be in that moment where I'm crying out to God while listening to my favorite music or playing my favorite lick on the guitar. Whatever place you have to cry out, I want you to take some time and go there now. As we condition our hearts and prepare that place as Go-To Guys and have things we need to get off our chest, we must go to that place of intimacy and push deeper. This includes being in total freedom with our Heavenly Father as we pursue complete freedom. Living from our identities and dreams requires us to continually look to stay free of lies we have agreed with. If you have things in your heart that may be keeping you from true freedom, there is no better time than right now to start. It is not by chance you have this book in your hands. God has this moment for you. Try not to kid yourself here. Be real. We are not perfect. Whatever you have hidden in your heart, the biggest sin or the smallest. Whatever you need to be free from. Take a moment in your place, and ask the Holy Spirit, "What area or thing do I need to get rid of to position myself for living out the freedom and destiny you have for me?" For once be quiet and listen. Just listen. Take a moment to listen and write down what the Holy Spirit gives to you as you ask. Whatever area or thing pops in your head, then write it down. For me it was pornography. Now lay it at the cross. I want you to say and fill in the blanks with what came to mind for you.

a. In the name of Jesus, I nail _____ to the cross. Insert the feeling or thought that is coming against you. There may be more than one.

b. I break all agreements I have made with _____, known or unknown, and I repent of joining with _____.

c. I ask you, Father, to send _____ away from me.

d. I ask you Father, what do you want to give me in place of _____?
-1-2-3 Skidoo Tool, Love After Marriage, pg. 78

The word you were given is God's promise to you. Every time you see red flags or the urge to go toward that agreement or sin, remember your word from God. Remember what He gave you and has for you instead of your sin. If you did not hear anything or have something pop up, ask again. Be sincere in your question and I promise God will be sincere in His answer.

Conditioning is not a one-time gym membership, or a short-lived commitment. Conditioning requires an attitude change. As we live out the biggest events and smallest events in our lives we need to be prepared. We as men must walk in freedom and authority over the battles we face. We must strive to place our conditioning above all else to prepare for the adventurous journey we are on. As we live free, we live vicariously through ourselves. Your life has already been filled with training and dedication whether you are young or old. It's how we choose to use that training that determines where we are going. No matter your age, we can all be Davids mastering our skills in the wilderness, preparing for the greatness God has for our lives . The approach is sometimes easy, sometimes hard. Regardless of the journey, we have to walk our own journeys with authentic God- given identities, ripe with extravagant dreams!

## *GO-TO GUY Response*

*"I believe all men have the ability to be Go-To Guys, if they are transparent before God and men. We are all given work to do on this earth. Some men just seem to be better postured to step into the work that God has for them. I believe that it is this posture or readiness of spirit that is open and sensitive to Gods leading that can sense when God is creating a divine appointment. This is also very attractive to others as they sense God in the Go-To Guy."*

*-Matt*

## THE GO-TO GUY

**2010 EVOLUTION TRAVERSE**

**MT. MENDEL**
37.1749° N. 118.6822° W

**SECTION TWO: THE ASCENT**

*I felt trapped by my job and the rat race, which can deflate a guy who just wants to be in the mountains running on a lonely trail to nowhere. This was also fueling our desire for this trip. We knew we had to press into the things placed in our hearts or we knew the devil would find a way to trap us further and keep us from pursuing our dreams.*

# INTRODUCTION TO SECTION 2

The way we bolted from Southern California, you would have thought we robbed a bank. Although there was much anticipation for this trip, there was also something deeper within us tugging at our hearts. Joe and I aspire to live in adventure, but sometimes I felt trapped by my job and the rat race, which can deflate a guy who just wants to be in the mountains running on a lonely trail to nowhere. This was also fueling our desire for this trip. We knew we had to press into the things placed in our hearts or we knew the devil would find a way to trap us further and keep us from pursuing our dreams. I believe this is where each of us has a Go-To Guy. For me, Joe is the man I can call and get riled and excited by just even talking about something we could conquer or accomplish. He inspires. Who is this Go-To Guy? Ironically I believe the answer lies deep in our own hearts. We pursue after the same things we desire to be. God places these men of God in our lives as examples and warriors that we can learn and walk out our faith with.

Most men can associate with the road trip. Now imagine a road trip, then getting to the trailhead to don a big pack, hike 10 miles over the Lamarck Col (over 13,000ft), then make base camp at 11,000ft, get up early to conquer the hardest traverse of your life, then bust your butt back to your base camp (assuming you can find it), do the same hike back out the next day to the car, and finally drive home to two beautiful wives. Yah, if only it was that simple.

Let me rephrase. This was epic! This is what we men are made for. This is part of the story line on the porch when we are old geezers. This was our time! All I can say is that our car ride into Bishop that day was filled with anticipation and desire.

We had forgotten our altitude medication, so we had my doctor call it in to Mojave, Ca. Wow; needless to say we walked into the funniest pharmacy in the middle of nowhere on the end of a strip mall. We then proceeded to watch as a lady argued about how her medication was wrong; how she "needed this, but actually got that." The old Chinese pharmacist and his daughter that were working were not budging. Then they all turned and looked at us. I told them what I was there for, got our prescriptions and left that dusty, particleboard pharmacy as the lady began her argument again. We headed for Bishop laughing and talking, going over route maps and descriptions.

Our plan included stopping and staying with Joe's sister who lived in Bishop. We were going to sleep on the couch when her roommate popped out this metal cot that they insisted Joe sleep on. One requirement for being a Go-To Guy: be able to sleep on hard, crappy surfaces and have enough pride to laugh it off and make people think you are tough. We could have slept on concrete that night. It wouldn't have mattered. We were so pumped for the climb that we could barely sleep. Except for one thing: we both took the altitude meds. We figured sleeping at 6,000ft the first night would be a good 24 hours of acclimatization, then we would hike to 13,000ft the next day and make base camp in the upper Darwin basin at 11,000ft. 0ft-13,000ft in 48 hours. No big deal right? Well, the meds were meant to curb our acclimatization and help us not get nauseous and sick with such a rapid descent. That could be a trip-ending event. The night in Bishop was interesting because the meds made me loopy. In retrospect I should have only had half the pill. However, I did not get sick, so something went right.

We awoke the next morning and proceeded to try and convince Joe's sister not to make us breakfast burritos. We had noticed things growing in their refrigerator the night before and we did not want to be hiking down the trail with explosive diarrhea. Joe took one for the team when he accepted his sisters' gift of a burrito with who-knows-what in it. We headed into town for a few last minute things then proceeded to drive to the Lamarck Lakes trailhead. As we were heading to the parking lot, we ran into the dad of some good friends of ours. It was a beautiful day. No clouds in the sky, sunny and bright blue.

The trailhead began at 9,500ft and we hiked up through the aspens and through the dense forest to the more open country that most associate the Sierra's with. We walked past lower Lamarck Lake and kept on through the super steep snowy section that climbs toward the Lamarck Col. Before you hike up the super steep couple hundred feet to the

Col, you come upon a true alpine style glacier lake. You can see straight through to the bottom and the glassy water is so cold it takes your breath away. We stopped to look back and revel at the 3,500ft gain we just did to 13,000ft, and the beautiful day it was down below in Bishop. We jumped on the snow and hiked the steps of snow up to the Lamarck Col. How amazing! Behind us lay the brown desert and the quick descent up through the various aspens, forests, and rocky alpine terrain. In front of us was Darwin Basin and directly across was the ridge for Evolution Traverse. It took our breath away! We were so excited. The trail comes and goes at this point, as technically there is no trail. For years many have travelled this way over the Col and so there are many trails leading toward the bottom of Darwin Canyon and the beautiful alpine lakes that fill the basin between these two ridges. We headed down and made use of the snowfields by riding our packs down the snow. It sure does go quick when you can slide on snow versus rock hop down a huge rock field. The sky was blue as we were talking up the ridge and pointing out the different peaks during the first part of the Traverse that we could see. We could also see Mt. Darwin where we were supposed to spend the night during the traverse. As we descended onto the basin floor, we made our way around the alpine lakes and headed toward the front of Darwin basin under the first unnamed peak on the traverse. This would be our base camp while we made the ascent of the traverse starting the next day. We only brought the tent fly and poles to make a shelter (to save weight) and got set up. One thing I had purchased at the store was a pound of chili and a packet of cheese. I was adamant with Joe that we should have a real meal before we embarked on two days of freeze dried food and bars. We cooked up the chili and then I dumped the cheese on top of the chili and we pigged out. About halfway through Joe mentioned to me jokingly that he is lactose intolerant. This is something I vaguely remembered from the past but it never really dawned on me. None-the-less he ate his portion and we crossed our fingers that there wouldn't be any explosions. We iced in the alpine lake we camped next to as well. What a way to ice! It was so cold but I put my whole body in! I was frozen but it felt so good on my muscles and legs. We watched the sun set with excitement as we put on warmer clothes and readied for bed. We would be getting up early to start up the huge initial ascent onto the traverse through the rock fall gully we camped near.

The ascent starts by going straight up from 11,250ft at base camp to 13,000ft then to the top of the first unnamed peak 13,360ft. It is straight through a major rock field and up some loose rock and even had some snow patches. We awoke and hiked with vigor as our excitement to finally be on this thing was here! We were flying up the gully. This is where we started joking about the altitude. We were living at sea level and two days later, we are going straight to 13,000ft! We were breathing hard but moving comfortably. Part of the uniqueness to ET besides the perfect granite in some sections is the constant route awareness that you have to maintain. You can easily get sidetracked by descending onto the wrong side of the ridge and get stuck, or by ascending the ridge only to find you could have come up a faster more direct route. The key is to keep moving and not get discouraged by a wrong move or by getting off route. If you stay true to the ridge, you are generally in the right place. When we got to the top of the first peak and felt the wind, it was breathtaking to look 360 degrees around and see that we truly were in the heart of Evolution basin. You could see the ending of the traverse and the peaks that we needed to follow. It looked truly daunting! The ridge had amazing drop offs as well that fell a couple thousand feet into the basins below. The ridge makes you appreciate everything you love about climbing and brings a sense of fulfillment and identity. I was so excited inside to be on the ridge and dropping down and up through huge boulders perched on cliffs. It was awesome to get on the ridge and start along. We wound along the ridge heading toward the second peak, Mt Mendel.

    As we were making our way along we came to a section that required us to make a decision on direction. We started one way down to the right toward Evolution Basin. As we progressed down this small outcropping, we had to wrap around it, back toward the ridge, but we realized it would have been twice as fast to go the other way. After a few of those you learn quickly that your judgment matters and counts up here. Wearing packs challenges you as well. Climbing and downclimbing is much different than just climbing with a harness on. I remember coming to this sloping section that was just loose rock and dirt. Down left was a good 1,000ft of ravine covered with a good section of dirty summer snow and runoff. As we slid on our butts and packs, you had to wonder whether there was a faster, better way. You start to wonder if the other side of the traverse would have been better to use. Some sections you just have to decide and go. You could spend all day standing there, trying to figure out which way to go. As we started to run low on water, we came to a place where there was some good melt-off coming straight off this rock. In-between each little shaded section and drop-off, we joked and talked our way through each section. We came to this huge pass where you could stand in the middle and look down on both sides. It was breathtaking minus the headwall we were about to free climb with packs on. We scaled up the section, only to get on a long sideways section of the next peak that seemed to go forever as a giant loose rock field. Each step was the realization we were near 13,000ft. We were breathing hard but moving good.

This ridge is truly unique in that you have to use a variety of climbing and mountaineering techniques to get around. You downclimb a wall, then ascend a boulder field, and then climb a little 15-foot section, only to drop through a crack system onto a small ledge that winds to the next section. It truly is a ridge with unexpected twists and turns. When we started the weather was perfect. It was cool and sunny with crystal clear blue skies. I should have known better. The calm before the storm.

## FIVE
# Basecamp

For those of you that have spent time in the mountains you know what I mean when I say the calm before the storm. It happens sometimes. This weird moment in a storm, right before it unloads. A storm needs lots of warm air mixed with moisture. This is the fuel for the engine. As the warm air is pulled in by the approaching storm, it makes its way through the storm cloud and makes its way toward the top of the storm cloud (updrafts). Once at the top the air ironically gets pulled down by the low pressure it left behind when it got sucked into the storm cloud. As this air descends back down, it happens to get warmer and drier, and as it turns out, happens to be the calm before the storm as it stabilizes an area. As science tells us, ascending air gets cooler and collects more moisture, whereas descending air tends to get warmer and drier. Now, since I just said all that. What the heck does that mean when you are stuck on a ledge at 13,000ft? It means you are about to wish you were at basecamp!

Basecamp is the safe haven, the refuge from the storm, a place to get healthy, a place to acclimate.

For Joe and I, it was setting up a basic tent, and dropping our main supplies at the base of Evolution Traverse. Basecamp could look like your home, or a mission base in Kenya. It could look like your cabin, or your dorm room. It could be your hotel room. It is that safe place we all have where we can get out of the driving weather, were we are protected. Where we can collect our breath and recharge. We have to learn what our basecamp looks like so we can recognize it when a storm is coming or find it when we are walking through a snowstorm. We have to cultivate it so that we have a place where we can recharge, get fed, be supplied, and garner the tools needed to accomplish our goals. Ultimately let's look at this place as the starting point; the beginning of the great adventure: the launch pad. If we are not afraid to go after our dreams and live our destinies, then why would we not want to have in place the mechanisms to establish basecamp and maintain it through our adventures!?

Here's how I see it. We need to be good in life at establishing a place where we can rest and recharge. I have watched many of my close friends make hard choices as they walk through tough times or deal with circumstances. Some of my friends have basecamps that look like a nuclear bomb went off. They have no point of rest in their life. Their camp is so tattered that they have no chance of weathering any type of storm. The hatches have been blown off. Their reservoir keeps getting drained. Other friends of mine however have done exceptionally well at creating around them an encampment that brings them rest, balances work and play, prepares them for the next adventure. They have created a place that gives them a great place to launch from. Basecamp is a form of our identity. It's a form of our core relationship in Christ. We need to establish, maintain, and prepare our basecamps, and as we do we will in turn see the fruits of that. I would venture to say that if we looked at different men and the basecamps they have, we could determine the health of their relationship in Christ by the health of their basecamp. Our relationship in Christ is a direct reflection of our basecamp. Does that make sense? We must learn to make a place for ourselves, and those in our circle, where we can operate from who we are. As we condition ourselves, we have to have a place that can protect us and keep us grounded.

How does David in the Bible run around in the desert running from cave to cave, his life in jeopardy, and still maintain his identity? He still cried out to God in those caves. He still walked in his integrity. He maintained the same authentic lifestyle, albeit from a cave. He knew that as long as He kept his focus in the right place, the Lord would honor him and give him the tools for success. I want to walk out a life where no matter where I go I can establish a place for me and my family that can weather the storm, prepare us for the calling God has for us, and spur us into that destiny. How do we do it you ask? Good question.

Basecamp is a work in progress. It is a place that takes time. As we grow in our identity I believe our basecamps begin to grow into the likeness of who we are and how we operate. It's important to see your basecamp as a continuation of ourselves, and all we need. It is a changing place, a waiting place. As we continue on in life there will be tools and resources that you will need to weather the next storm or battle. This is where discernment becomes an integral part of the Go-To Guy and one of the most important aspects of your basecamp. Expedition teams prepare and plan for every conceivable thing, whether good or bad, to happen. They use their discernment as they look at weather and routes, to determine what they will need to accomplish their goals. We have to see our basecamp as a place of learning and growing. You'd better be comfortable in your basecamp because sometimes God has us in a place of waiting. People who operate from a tattered basecamp seem miserable to me. They are beat up. Less rested. Fighting to stay even remotely connected. Instead of discerning what lies ahead, they are fighting just to stay afloat; to survive.

In the Go-To Guys I have observed, I see them able to discern what red flags look like in their life. Using that discernment, they break their routine and move away from areas that would tear them down, into areas that promote growth. They step toward the challenge. Learning to discern can keep us moving in the right direction. It's important to read and see the clues around us. You could be picking up something in the Spirit around you, or you could be having a horrible morning. Whatever the case, you have a choice to keep making agreements with what you are experiencing or you can break free. By breaking free, I mean changing the atmosphere around you. You are discerning what is tearing you down and choosing to fight for more of His presence. As we do this we promote our basecamps into a healthy place. It fosters a lifestyle constantly seeking after the things that will keep drawing you into a deeper revelation with Christ and ultimately a deeper relationship with Him.

As we learn to discern red flags in our lives, we can learn how to stop the direction we are going and realign ourselves to the direction God has for us. For myself, and some of my closest friends, worship is a key ingredient for realigning with our purpose. We can choose to stay where we are, and try to do the typical guy response through things. Meaning: grunt, tear, and tough our way through something; or we can do what one of the toughest men ever to walk the planet did. David may have been hunted by Saul, but his integrity remained intact. His basecamp provided him the tools he needed to survive the onslaught. Here was a man who was running from place to place, his life in jeopardy. He acted crazy in front of Achish king of Gath, escaped to hide in caves, moving from place to place, ended up in the Desert of Ziph. Eventually in the Desert of En Gedi,

Saul catches up with David and his men. As Saul is relieving himself in a cave, David cuts a piece of his robe. Then David confronts Saul. How does a man running for his life continue to maintain a basecamp worthy of a King?! David, even in the midst of his trial continues to pursue the Lord in all aspects of his life, in every situation and cave that he ended up in! David knew who he was. He knew what his calling and destiny was. He knew what God had for him and he positioned himself to be ready. He worshipped. He listened. He was prepared to run when he needed to and ultimately face Saul when it was time.

We must get on our faces. Unload our junk at the cross. Then Worship. Unabashed worship. I have found that as I worship, the devil really tries to come on hard. He tries everything he can to distract me from worshipping our God. Why? Because he knows we are about to shift the atmosphere. As we worship we align our spirit to His. We draw deeper in our love as we commune with Holy Spirit. What happens after that worship is what scares the devil and what he hates the most. We are reenergized and refocused to walk the path God has for us. I believe this is the most important aspect to maintaining your basecamp. Whether you are in some remote base in Mozambique, or on the streets in Chicago, or grinding away at work, we must learn to discern our situations and makes shifts in our spirit attitudes so that we can be ready for when the storm clears and the next adventure begins. We tend to be hit with opposition when we least expect it.

Like the calm before the storm, we need to be able to discern when a storm is approaching. We need to be able to recognize when warm air is about to slam into a pocket of cold moist air and create the perfect storm. As we move through life we will inevitably weather many storms, but how we discern them and move on from them determines much about who we are as men. As you prepare your basecamp, utilize the tools God has given you. Be discerning and deliberate in your planning. You will never be able to plan for all that life has, instead, we have to learn to recognize when it may be time to move or time to be in a holding pattern. We have to recognize when we need to refocus or stay the course. What I have seen in the Go-To Guys in my life is the humility to lay it all down at Jesus' feet. In turn, I have watched as we honor our Father and refocus to His will, that He is faithful to encourage, refocus us, reenergize us, and send us deeper into the unknown than ever before. The Go-To Guy uses his basecamp as the stepping off point for his destiny. It fuels his destiny and journey. As we learn to seek after the Fathers heart, He fortifies our walls, encourages our hearts, and gives us purpose. For the sake of your basecamp and the future of your life, lets be men who can use our basecamp as a place where we can get excited about where we are and what we are about to accomplish. Lets use it as a safe place where rest comes easy and dreams run wild. Lets press in for more discernment from Papa Daddy and seek to always see the calm before the storm as inviting!

## GO-TO GUY Response

I have been thinking about your question, especially yesterday and this morning. My wife has really felt the spiritual oppression here and was feeling discouraged and I was a bit of a grump yesterday after riding in the moving truck squished for 8 hours. So in a way we got off track... the reason why we are here...the focus was on ourselves and not to bless the Smiths. So we worshipped in our hotel room for about 45 minutes this morning. After proclaiming His promises over this place, over the people and what He wanted to do through us, we were definitely refocused, reenergized, and ready to rock and roll. So definitely worship realigns my thinking and priorities with Gods plan for that hour, day, week year, etc. It caused a shift of the heart and mind and also enables one to realize the power of Christ in us to do His work, which causes an excitement that should be illegal.

I was also thinking about my running and because it is fairly mindless, as opposed to soccer or volleyball where a full engagement is necessary, it enables one to connect to God. Many times I have received inspiration and visions while on runs. So this is definitely a basecamp for me, especially exploratory runs like the one this morning.

*When I explore I don't get tired I actually am fueled on endorphins. So a key here I think is breaking out of a routine, engaging in a challenge that enables a man to see that he's still got it, and then that enables him to apply that confidence to other areas of life. I remember when my brother and I ran up Mt. Whitney, accomplishing that physical feat enabled me to enter the battle zone of teaching in the inner city school system with drugs, gangs, and violence as the norm. Interestingly enough it was the outdoors that broke the ice with those students as I took them camping, hiking, mt. biking, and snowboarding.*
*–Jason*

# SIX
# Attitude for Altitude

How do we as men live the life of the overcomer? How do we maintain an attitude that ultimately will determine our altitude for the rest of our lives? I have been captivated recently by probably one of the most crucial special operations stories in the Bible. It determined the direction and plight for an entire nation. Imagine Moses coming to you and asking you to go into a new land (the land promised to you by God) to spy out the land, the people, how the cities are built, and the fruit. All the leaders of the Tribes of Israel were sent out, twelve in all. This is the first time we see Caleb in the Bible. He is forty years old. Commissioned to spy out the land promised to the Israelites. After forty days of exploring out the land, you return to Kadesh (where the entire community of Israelites were) to report what you had found. The report is what is fascinating! This is where I want to dive into what it means to have an attitude of an overcomer; by looking at the ordinary life of Caleb and his extraordinary attitude and how it led him to a place only worthy of the calling as a Go-To Guy.

Imagine yourself as you begin to share of what you found in this big Promised Land; surrounded by thousands as they listen and see what you brought back. You speak of how vast and big the cities are, how fortified their walls are, the enormity of their crops and fruit. You then begin to share that the people who live there are powerful and you begin to insight fear and doubt into the people surrounding you as you share with Moses. "Then Caleb silenced the people before Moses and said, we should go up and take possession of the land, for we can certainly do it." (Numbers 13:30). You pipe up though and begin to spread a bad report about the land you just spent forty days spying on. The entire night the nation of Israel weeps, and fear and doubt sweeps through the tribes. Then as Moses and Aaron fall flat on their faces, Joshua and Caleb stand tall and declare once again what was promised them by God. This time, you and those around begin to talk of stoning them. Then in the middle of all the chaos, God's glory fills that tent place. Imagine the atmosphere. Here you are standing in a huge meeting, all these chosen men who have just returned from forty days, the Israelites in complete disbelief, and only two guys standing in the whole place ready to be stoned for their convictions and beliefs in what God has promised them. Ah, the Go-To Guy reveals himself. I love it. What can we take from the life and attitude of a man like Caleb? I want to look at his life, his unwavering devotion to be that guy, the one who stands tall, above all else to Glorify God and put Him first.

> *"He was not an Abraham, nor a Moses, nor a David, nor a Paul. He was just Caleb, a man out of the common run of folks, living a life brilliant in no other respect than in its faith, obedience and courage. He was an ordinary man living an extraordinary life not because of anything in him or in his circumstances but solely because of his relationship to his God. Caleb became nothing that God might become everything. Caleb had but one concern, his relationship to his God. That being right everything else must be right. Caleb went in a straight line allowing no deflection or deviation. In youth and in old age, amid all difficulties and discouragements, in face of all opposition, he wholly followed the Lord...Canaan stands for the Christian's deliverance from all the power of Satan, for his full inheritance of all his possessions in Christ, for his enjoyment of the peace and power of a Spirit-filled life. God teaches us through Caleb how such a life may be obtained and maintained. Caleb calls and challenges us to enter into it". "Let us go up at once and possess it: for we are well able to overcome it."*
> *- Ruth Paxson, Caleb the overcomer*

If ever there was a guy in the Bible who emulates the Go-To Guy, this is it. An example of the attitude

God calls us to cannot be seen any better than with this ordinary man Caleb. The Go-To Guy is a dreamer. A lover. A fighter. The attitude Caleb walked out his entire life shows us how he dreamed of nothing but the presence with his God. It is mentioned six times in the Bible that Caleb, "wholly followed the Lord (Joshua 14:14)." Wholly. Unwavering. He was the man that stood with Joshua and gave good report. Think of this. You go out to spy out a land with all the leaders. There has to be some camaraderie between these men. There has to be some loyalty. There has to be some bond that held these men together through all the trials and being led out of Egypt. The difference lies in that Caleb did not see his past and Egypt and all the trials they had overcome as his strength. They were promises built upon promises that were encouraging Caleb in the ultimate fact in his heart: God promised us this land. Therefore, to Caleb, the battle has already been won. So it stands that it is easy for a man to follow his steadfast heart and go against his brothers. He gave good report that day and into the night. It must have broken his heart to see the disbelief, fear, and doubt in his people. They believed that God had brought them all through the desert, led them out of Egypt, only to die at the hand of giants! Caleb believed it was just God fulfilling his promise. He already knew that the battle had been won. He already knew that this land was their inheritance. Caleb gave good report in all truth. He did not diminish one bit from the enormity of the cities and the people. Here's the difference however. Caleb was able to glorify and magnify the Lord through what he saw. Caleb believed that the power and presence of the Lord in them and with them would defeat anything against them. He walked through that land with the enemy already broken and defeated in his mind. He was probably already dreaming about what it would be like to inhabit this land. What an attitude of being an overcomer!

The Go-To Guy lives from this mindset. Our circumstances must not determine our life. Our attitude and mindset of the overcomer must determine our lives. We should operate our lives looking forward to the inheritance and promises from the Lord. What I love most about the Go-To Guy is that he is unhesitant in decisions because his assurance comes from things not seen but unseen. His assurance comes from God's word and obeying what ultimately is in his heart. Caleb lived with no fear. Why? Because he already knew that God won. "Wholly followed the Lord (Numbers 32:12)." Caleb wholly followed the Lord. I can think back to so many times where I was so grateful to have that man in my life that could stand up, believe in what he believes in, and walk with that assurance. It encourages me to do the same and trust in my relationship with Christ instead of any preconceived notion that I could come up with a better plan. It teaches us to look ahead, anticipate that our victory is already won. To not fear walking it out to fruition. As we look further at Caleb, watch what happens.

So here is Caleb and Joshua, the only two men that God allows to live after the whole spying debacle. We talk about how we are sometimes in a desert and that God is silent, or trying to teach us through our desert. But I wonder if we look at Caleb in this time if that holds true? Here is a man that has to wander through the desert with a bunch of unbelieving, murmuring, bitter people. One by one they are falling down dead, funeral after funeral Caleb has to go to. 40 years of misery and turmoil. Wandering around in circles, day after day. Its one thing to be the man that stands in the heat of the battle like David and strike down the Philistine, or in Caleb's instance to defy the masses and their attitudes of unbelief. But, what about a lifelong pursuit of steadfast devotion to God? We have talked in previous chapters about positioning ourselves for the long haul, the life of integrity. Well here it is plain as day as Caleb walks around the desert for forty years. Instead of enjoying what he knows is his in the Promised Land, he is stuck wandering with his people because of their sin and punishment.

I'm often presented with the common line, "Well its just not the same. You have never dealt with what I have, so until you go through what I have been through, you couldn't possibly understand." Really? I feel the attitude here is one of self-pity and defeat. I believe the Go-To Guy represents and shows through his life how to have the attitude of the overcomer.

One who not only can stand up in the moment, but also one who can stand the tests of time. A life that can be looked back upon and remembered as one that, "wholly followed the Lord (Joshua 14:14)."

Caleb spent his middle years wandering around with the Promised Land on his mind. Everyday was a battle to see God provide manna, while in the back of his mind were the thoughts of the huge abundances in the Promised Land. Instead, war, fatigue, marching around in circles was all he saw. In spirit this man was sold out to God. Like some of us, he was probably thinking what a waste! To a man with total devotion it must have seemed quite futile to be wandering around when he could have been sowing the seeds from his rightful place and inheritance from the Lord. The scene must have been really upbeat those forty years! How does the Go-To Guy stand even this arduous battle of 40 years of nothing? How does he bypass the horrible attitudes, the death, and the depression? How does he prevail from the fray and mind numbing existence that I'm sure the devil leapt for joy over? I'm sure Caleb was alone as well. There was no way a bunch of people were going to come over to Caleb and strike up a conversation about the land they turned from because of their attitudes and rebellion. There was no way they were going to talk about that supposed land with Caleb, who loved it and talked so passionately about it!? No, I bet Caleb was very much alone in his desert. Enter this Go-To Guy.

There was nobody in this situation, except maybe Joshua, that could even understand what it meant to have so much devotion and love for something believed so tangible and given by God. Caleb saw, smelled, and probably tasted it. He was witness to the amazing land God promised. Was that going anywhere from Caleb's mind? This man had to set aside any thought of bitterness and resentment toward his people for their rebellion. He waited patiently. I'm sure it wasn't easy. Instead he shows us his authentic spirit that he carries (Joshua 14: 6-15). Much like Caleb looked forward, believing in what his inheritance was in the land when he spied it, he also spent forty years looking forward to what was promised to him by God. Having the attitude of the overcomer he was able to reach out with all that he had physically and spiritually to see what was going to be his inheritance. He never lost sight of his faith.

> *"The remembrance of God's promise to him; the consciousness of God's presence with him and the assurance of God's delight in him sustained and strengthened Caleb. Working in obedience to God, he had fellowship with God. So he had the rest of Canaan in his heart, before he had it in his life."* -Ruth Paxson Caleb the Overcomer

The final piece of Caleb's life is this. Here he is in his old age. This Go-To Guy goes through his whole life completely devoted to God. Most men get to retirement and begin to relax. Many feel a bit of a letdown as they begin to relax and enjoy the fruits of their life. I don't think Caleb relaxed for one second. This man instead of coming down from a full life continued on.

*"As yet I am as strong this day as I was in the day that Moses sent me; as my strength was then, even so is my strength now, for war, both to go out and to come in."* JOSH. 14:11.

Truly authentic to the core is Caleb. His attitude and strength continue at 85 years old as they did in his young days! God's promises and presence never left him; in fact it only strengthened his resolve. As we see below this man walks right up and says: "Give me this mountain!" Nothing had changed for him. He knew it was his then, and knew it was his in his late age! He never waivered from his attitude and even wanted to go to war as an old man! Most guys his age would be rolling up in a wheelchair to fight, but not this Go-To Guy.

"Now therefore give me this mountain, of which the Lord spoke in that day; for you heard in that day how the Anakims were there, and that the cities were great and fenced; if so be the Lord will be with me, then I shall be able to drive them out, as the Lord said." JOSH. 14:12.

As we look at what it means to be men with rock solid attitudes, we must remember having an upright attitude goes much farther than just one situation or scenario. Like Caleb shows us, it is possible to have a life of a positive can-do attitude. As we see, it keeps him in a place where he comes fully alive through his destiny! Even to the point that as an old man he is just as strong and accomplishing just as much as he did when he was young. Oh how we could learn from such a Go-To Guy!

> *"One resolve seems to have been paramount all through his life—to keep his own life up to standard so that God could delight in him and would never have to deprive him of His presence."* -Ruth Paxson, Caleb the Overcomer

> *"What you look for you will find & where you look you will end up going."* –Christine Caine of Hillsong

Caleb's gaze never left that Promised Land. Never. His attitude never changed toward his goal. Not once. How do we as men maintain a standard as high as Caleb? By doing what this godly man did. We do everything possible to be resolute in keeping ourselves as close as possible to our loving Savior. We keep our sacred romance with Him as near and dear as possible. We will maintain his presence ensuring that we are constantly feeding from the real source in our Lord. How do we become a man willing to stand in front of tens of thousands of people to give a positive report? By knowing deep within ourselves who we are and the attitude we should present.

I want to be that man that can stand the test of time. I want to fix my gaze on the promises of God's word, seeking out His presence. I want to stand with my men in full upright integrity with no doubts. I want to achieve everything for my Lord. I want to change my attitude to that of Caleb's with every intention of laying my abilities at the cross and focusing on one truth: it's all about God. Our achievements and altitude in this life are directly related to our ability to lay it before Him. If you are one of the 10 spies and looking for impossible things, then surely you will find those. But, if you are willing to be in the minority, to be the Go-To Guy, you will find your destiny has an altitude with no ceiling. What we look for we will inevitably find. As we glorify God and seek His presence, fixing our gaze on the unseen, we will see impossibilities as possible. We will soar with wings as eagles. We will be walking with an attitude of Caleb. You will be one "who wholly followed the Lord. (Josh 4:9)" Attitude for altitude. What's your altitude?

## GO-TO GUY Response

*I've had many experiences in life where my Go-To Guy was a vital part of the outcome. In particular, when I was 18 years old, my girlfriend told me she was pregnant. I was terrified and knew that I had to tell my father. He was my Go-To Guy. Although I wasn't sure what his response would be, he exhibited the peace of God in my storm, loved me no matter what, and guided me through the process of becoming a father. I look back and see how influential he has been in my ability to father my children in the ways of God. I'm thankful my Go-To Guy was there and I hope to be the same for others. I have definitely been blessed to have a Go-To Guy. I'm not sure I would be living a Godly life without him. He has impacted me more than any other man on the planet.*

*–Josh*

## SEVEN
# Off Route

Think back to a time where you really screwed up. Maybe you lied to your wife. You got caught cheating in college. Maybe you stole something, went to jail. It could have been an affair, or maybe you just went through a nasty divorce. Maybe you are just one of those guys that every time you go into the woods to go camping, you seem to get lost and the National Guard gets called to come find you! Regardless, we all seem to get off route sometimes. What I have noticed in the Go-To Guy is this uncanny ability to set aside the pride and ego, get on his knees, and recognize the need for forgiveness. It's not a sign of weakness to be forgiven. In fact it takes an even bigger man to admit his wrongdoing, and set it straight.

On Evolution Traverse, there were many times where I'm sure we were off route. But if you stay near the ridge, you will find your way. How true it is as well as we wind our way through the ridge of life. We can get as much discernment and wisdom as we want, but in the end there will be mistakes that cause us to go off route. I could write a whole book on being off route it seems. Even the Go-To Guy makes mistakes, gets off course, but it's how he stays true to the ridge of life that dictates his direction.

    Every man somewhere inside wants to feel significant in this world. That he makes a difference. In an effort to be real, I'll share my struggles with exaggeration. I exaggerate. I can stretch the smallest thing into the largest. My need to exaggerate comes from needing to feel significant. My exaggerating and lying was also a habit formed to cover my long struggle with porn. I had a dream about lying one time. It freaked me out. It was in a time when God was speaking truth deeply to me. In the dream the word liar was burning on the wall. Parts of it were smoldering and re-lighting. I felt like I lied and exaggerated about everything because it was a smoke screen of what makes me look better in the eyes of others. It was my need for self worth. It stemmed out of keeping a secret; my porn secret. Talk about getting off route! I was getting the need met somewhere else. Ask any of my close friends and they will tell you I can stretch things. Really far. How embarrassing. My pride was so big I couldn't even see how silly I looked to my closest friends and how they saw in me the needs I had!

    Pride can be a killer and a huge brick wall in our efforts to come clean about something or to get back on track. It seems pride can dictate our entire life if we let it. It can cause us to say things we never thought possible. Pride can make our actions do something we never imagined was possible. As we get off route in life, like my exaggerating and lying, it is a rabbit trail that seems to go off into the abyss. Have you ever felt totally lost? For some it only takes a small thing to get us back on track with God. For me it takes an act of Congress to get me to realize the magnitude of my problem. Probably a direct reflection of how large my pride and ego is!

I want to make sure we understand each other here. This book is for all of us to recognize what we all have as potential inside, dictated to us by men who are ahead of us in the journey or walking it out with us. I'm asking here for you to take a good look at yourself; to truthfully and unashamedly take a good look at yourself. That is the goal here. There are times where I know I am off route. It is frustrating. It's frustrating to know you are in a hard position and everything in us as men says to push through. Everything inside us says to grit our teeth, retreat to the cave, hunker down, to prepare for war. Why is this the response we gravitate toward? This attitude affects everything. Those around us start to run and hide. Men can be brutal. It's like the downward slide is all we can do to cope with the situation we may be dealing with. We get way off route.

What sends me over the deep end sometimes is so ridiculous. I was hiking through the snow yesterday with my wife and newborn. Instead of it being a beautiful crystal clear Idaho day, it was a sludge up a hill through deep-crusted snow. I didn't say a word till we got to the top. My wife can always recognize where I'm at. It seems my cave can tear down those around me as well. She always tries to bring me back, to encourage me. She is the victor of grace through Christ that I always fail to see. I was feeling pressure about where we were at with direction for our new little family. I just wanted to scream because I feel so trapped and helpless in this situation. Enter the Go-To Guys in my life.

Let me tell you something about surrounding yourself with Go-To Guys. Find some men. Find some men you trust and let them in. Be in relationship with them. Because when the crap hits the fan, and it will, you will be surrounded by men who can help encourage you. Men who can build you up in only the way you can hear and understand. They will know you. They will recognize, just like your wife or close relatives, when something will be amiss in your life. No matter what, position yourself to have these men in your life with a direct line to you. David and Jonathon encouraged each other. They knew each other on a deep level. They recognized when things were off route. One of the mighty warriors in my life, showed up in the midst of all this yesterday. I got on the phone with my best friend and was just blah. I usually tend to just focus on what's going on with him and deflect all questions that come my way if I'm struggling with something. After our conversation he texted me with a word that I have kept close to my heart and encourage other men with:

"Man just want to say how impressive it is to hear the peace in your voice during this season. It speaks of such a strong faith and closeness of Him in your life during circumstances that average men could not handle. I'm praying with you in this season but I already know it's going to be better than we both could imagine. Thank you for your deep wisdom and encouragement. Here is a word for you- Clean your Sword. After you have done battle a warrior needs to clean and sharpen his blade; it is just as important as the use of it. It is a time of reflection seeing the blood of the enemy in victory and polishing the battered edge preparing for the next encounter. I've had a lot of lessons learned this way. Love you brother. Keep up the good fight. Hell doesn't stand a chance against you." -Joe

Wow. I stood there speechless for a moment. Here is a man willing to encourage me in truth, not in what I was believing. I was choosing to make agreements with my circumstance and believe where I was. Joe saw the truth and chose to encourage me from where we are in Christ, not the world. This is the shift. Encouragement during a tough time can sometimes get shot down. What I mean is this. Men sometimes tend to deflect encouragement or any kind of word from others that would try to help us or build us up. We tend to think that it's only going to come from us, that the answer lies somewhere in us. What I love about the Go-To Guy is that when he is off route, there is a red flag in his mind and the process of being teachable begins, and brings reconciliation if we are willing to listen. If we are willing to listen. That's not a typo. It is here again for this. God places these men in our lives if we are willing to be vulnerable and open to be taught and listen to what is being spoken over us. Yes, you have a choice. You can choose to continue on in your rant or poutiness, you can be angry all you want. You can choose to ignore it all, deflect it all, one up it all. But if you position these men in your life, you'd better be ready to hear what they have to say! You had better be ready to accept the truth from men who are appointed to be in your life. My best bud spoke out exactly where I was. He knew it without us even talking about it. This is why we must have these men in our lives.

The Go-To Guy uses being off route to his advantage, and ultimately to get back on track. Here's what I mean. We have talked about being overcomers, dreaming big, living from our identities, and what it means to walk those out in our lives. But when we get off route, it seems we no longer live from those dreams or identities that are so God given. The devil plays us and gets us to meander through these random rabbit trails that keep us from being on route to our destinies. Our situations rarely change, but our perspectives of those situations is what dictates our direction. As I have seen it, the Go-To Guys in my life have shown me that it takes an extremely humble man, to get on his knees and give up. Yes give up. Most men see giving up as a sign of weakness. In fact giving up is quite the opposite. As we surrender to the Lord, we give to him our burdens, and we come under His authority in our lives. We align ourselves to His purpose and destiny. We drop to our knees and humbly bow before Him letting it all go. That's not easy as a man. I have seen the Go-To Guy make a complete 180-degree turn in his life right in front of me. Pride keeps going and going, driving us deeper down the wrong road, and then all the sudden the Go-To Guy says wait a second, I'm not laying this down and allowing God to have complete authority in my life. I'm driving my own car. As we lay down at the cross being off route, it positions us to come back under God's authority and that includes His covering. As we do this, we can start to see clearly what God is trying to teach us. The fog begins to lift from the road. The turns begin to straighten out; the bumpiness begins to fade to smooth roads. We start to get excited and dream again. There is light at the end of the tunnel. We are on route again roping up for the next climb.

Imagine yourself running along a beautiful trail along a beautiful river. As you run along with your favorite music pumping in your headphones, you notice up ahead that the trail starts to veer up against a wet, rocky cliff. You see moss hanging down and running water coming down. As you run towards it you see that the trail runs right into a tunnel. It is dark and you can't see the light on the other side.

As you get closer you have a choice. You can turn around, or you can venture in the tunnel. You decide to keep going. You run your hand along the cold damp rock wall that makes up the tunnel. As you keep running, you run your hand along the wall as a guide. The floor is wet and water drops on your head as you continue along. In the distance you see a small circle of light. As you keep running, the light is getting bigger and bigger. You begin to see the end of the tunnel. Instantly you burst back out onto the small single-track trail. It is still following the river, but more beautiful on this side. There are more trees and plants, sunlight flickering through the canopy of trees above. As you continue on, you notice another tunnel up ahead. This time it is easier to run in. You already know what to expect. It is still dark, but you have more confidence as you run through this one. Tunnel by tunnel you run for miles. Each tunnel you come to gets shorter and easier to run through. As you come to the end of this tunnel, you immediately are out in a huge green valley. You can see a beautiful barn at the end of the valley. Vineyards are shaping the hills with your trail now becoming a small two-lane dirt road winding toward a mountain pass. Our journeys are winding and full of dark tunnels, but its how we see, when we can't see at all, that determines our ultimate destination. We can choose to turn around when we can't see the destination or we feel like we can't keep going. But if we continue into the adventure choosing to enter into the dark unknown tunnel, we are taken on a journey, brought back on route, and shown the promised destined land.

I would encourage you to look closely to the times in your life where you have been off route. As we can see, we must continue to align ourselves in a place where we are not afraid to step into the unknown. Where we can confidently walk through the unknown tunnels of life seeking our destiny. Being able to maintain the Go-To Guy inside of us as we run through the unknown is a challenge we can all believe in. How we stay true to the direction God has placed in us, and maintain our hearts to stay on course even when off route, is the defining character of the Go-To Guy. I look forward to running the tunnels and ridges of life. We may fall off or get lost, but if we keep our hearts in tune and focused, I have no doubt we will reach that awesome destination God has for our lives . I am confident the Lord will keep showing you and enticing you into that next unknown tunnel. Stay focused, stay direct, and keep Him close. Keep running Go-To Guy.

*Return to your rest, oh my soul…* Psalm 116:7

### *GO-TO GUY Response*

"The Go-To Guy is someone, possibly a best friend, who has come to your rescue OR was in a difficult predicament with you and helped overcome this challenge. An overcomer and a victor. The Go-To Guy has the ability to make the best decision under the worst scenario and live with the decision."

*-Dennis*

EIGHT

# The Direct Route

As a climber there is always talk about the direct route when I'm roping up for a climb. It is the shortest route and distance between two navigational points; usually the direct path to the chains (the top of your route). As you progress as a climber, you go from a climbing grade of 5.8 or 5.9 to climbing very hard 5.13 or 5.14 routes. Routes toward the 5.8 range tend to have many holds and variations that can be done up one particular climb. As you progress through the climbing grades, routes become more and more intentional. You have to do very specific moves to make it past certain sections. It becomes more and more direct, with holds becoming very sparse and getting smaller and smaller. Once at the 5.13 to 5.14 grade, you are committing to very specific moves and usually have to do a route one particular way to reach the top.

Isn't it funny that Caleb in the Bible remained one way his whole life to reach the top? He spent his whole life doing different routes, progressing through harder and harder sequences and yet, maintained the right moves through the most intense parts of his life to reach the top. He knew what moves God was requiring of him and climbed that way his whole life. Staying focused on Caleb for a moment, how did he manage to stay on the direct route his entire life, even as the Israelites disbelief and fear caused so much extra wandering around for him? We only see his life in the Bible start at age 40, but he enters the Bible as the chief of his tribe. I doubt his childhood and upbringing was anything but impressive. You don't get to that position in life without showing some very specific qualities that guide you to a place of trust and honor to lead people. Then we watch as he walks through life, literally, always keeping his direct route in spirit to the Promised Land! Even as the tribes of Israel wandered around the wilderness as punishment for their fear and disbelief, Caleb still maintained the direct route in his heart. Getting off route happens but I want to look at what it means for us as men to stay on the direct route.

On Evolution Traverse Joe and I had poured over many a blog about the route we needed to take. As best we could, we tried to seek out every piece of advice we could get about the traverse. Even though you are on a ridge, the beauty of the traverse is; the ability to make good decisions to guide you quickly and directly through each section of ascents and drops. We found early that morning on the traverse the discernment needed to make fast, good, decisions that ultimately guided us. Even for seasoned climbers, this type of climbing can discourage you. Usually after taking a few wrong turns, you quickly come to the realization you cannot continue making those mistakes. You change course, make adjustments, and continue on staying positive. Like we talked about in the last chapter, we often find ourselves getting off route. What I want to look at is how we stay on the direct route. If the Go-To Guy gets off track, we have seen how he can get back, but I'm talking about how do we live the life of Caleb? How do we stay one that, "wholly followed the Lord"(Joshua 4:9) our entire life?

I have no doubt God uses our off route choices to help us grow, and prepare us for the next tunnels and adventures he has for us. What about making choices that keep us on the direct route? I believe the Go-To Guy emulates this well. What can we do to make healthy choices that direct us along the ridge of life? In Go-To Guys I have watched, one thing is sure: wisdom, wisdom, wisdom. Learning how to be a son, listening, learning, and the gentle reminder that wisdom rests solidly on the fear of the Lord. Proverbs 2:1-11 is the epitome of staying on the direct route.

> *"My son, if you accept my words and store up my commands within you, turning your ear to wisdom and applying your heart to understanding, and if you call-out for insight and cry aloud for understanding, and if you look for it as for silver and search for it as*

*for hidden treasure, then you will understand the fear of the Lord and find the knowledge of God. For the Lord gives wisdom and from his mouth come knowledge and understanding. He holds victory in store for the upright, he is a shield to those whose walk is blameless, for he guards the course of the just and protects the way of his faithful ones. Then you will understand what is right and just and fair—every good path. For wisdom will enter your heart, and knowledge will be pleasant to your soul. Discretion will protect you, and understanding will guard you."*

You would never scale Mt. Everest without first spending years of climbing, years of preparing, and years of planning. As you pour over weather patterns, you study those who have gone before you to glean what wisdom you can from them. You take in all the "beta" you can, the pertinent info, as we say in the climbing world. You look at all the successful teams that made it. You then study the unsuccessful teams to see what went wrong. You use both as a way to better prepare. You see the right information can save your life in the mountains. I believe Solomon was calling young men to listen. But what exactly does it mean to walk out the direct route. How do we stay the course set before us, designed by God himself?

The Go-To Guy is multifaceted; a Leatherman of sorts. The MacGyver of his time; the go-go gadget man. What makes the Go-To Guy the most interesting man in the world is that he has learned and operated many different tools garnered from his life. David didn't just learn how to use a sling and a rock. He knew how to be bold and brave. He knew what danger was and how to confront it. He knew what it meant to be calm amidst the storm. He was discerning. David's life began to unfold after he slay that giant man. All his years of training as a boy, broke into his destiny and calling over his life. As he walked out his purpose, we see the story unfold.

The direct route is the culmination of many things as we see what it means to be that guy. Why is it so hard for a man to ask for wisdom on something? Why is it so hard to cry aloud for it and call-out for insight? The direct route is staying on course. It requires a life of utmost dedication and integrity. It requires of us the confidence to make decisions. It calls from us to be the man not afraid to call out for more wisdom. Our lives must mirror that of Caleb and the life of integrity. Maintaining the direct route requires of us to live bold and unafraid. We must be willing as men to make the hard choices and walk out the hard things because we know down deep they are the right things to do. Caleb maintained his focus on God, never wavering. Even amidst others around you being off route and walking out lives void of integrity and honor, we must be the guy that stands alone among the crowd; confident in our choices and decisions, knowing they are not based on the world's view but heaven's view here on earth.

You see, the Go-To Guy will make mistakes, but will always stay near to the direct route because he knows the value of being upright and blameless. It looks different for sure. Not safe. Wild as Christ can be! God shields, guards, and protects us as we walk this razor sharp route. It requires more of us. It is not easy. As we learn to walk blameless and pure, and guard wisdom, we take stock and value from all that we are willing to listen to. As we accept hard words from close friends, and store up the commands in the Bible, we begin to walk as Jesus did.

Why is it that at your work you have a guy that seems to always have the favor with your boss? You know what I'm talking about. It's that guy who isn't afraid to say no to the boss, has some boundaries, and is respected by coworkers. They are different. It's interesting, the old saying, "Keep your friends close, and your enemies closer." Very successful businessmen know how to spot upright men, Christian or not. Their life is a walking, talking example of what it means to have honor and integrity. The boss just knows from years of business that this guy is trustworthy and blameless. The Lord protects those who are faithful. Are you faithful right now in your circumstances? Are you walking the direct route at work or church? What if you sought after your relationship in Christ like you do for that next thing you want to buy? What if you cried aloud for wisdom much like the desire you had for that next promotion? You see, we can be the guy in the office that is known for being upright, being bold, being unafraid, trustworthy to the core. As we look for God like buried treasure, and desire Him above all else, we will then begin to understand the fear of the Lord and find His knowledge. He will guide us and protect us. We will maintain the direct route. We will be unwavering in our approach to succeed in our endeavors.

When I was in the Navy I was as low as they come on the totem pole. However, it seemed that the Lord kept placing me in positions that were way above my pay grade. I was actually going into situations where I was seen as the Go-To Guy for decisions and situations that were only filled with ranking officers. In fact, it came to a point where I was being used as an advisor and assistant to one of the directors of my command! Here is one of the highest ranks listening to one of the lowest ranks. For some reason the Lord kept placing me in positions of authority and trust. After the Navy, I was hired by a very successful business as a manager in the same field. I came in only knowing in my heart what I needed to say and do. I really had no idea what I was doing, but God showed me every step of the way. I trusted that my decisions were sound. Immediately I started an amazing relationship with the CEO and although one of the lowest on the totem pole, was used to make very big decisions that dictated the direction the business went. My decisions even trumped my boss in some circumstances. God protected me so many times when it seemed my decision or circumstance would overtake me. I was amazed at how much favor poured out. He was protecting His faithful one. God uses the least of these for the greatest good. Reread the verses we just read in Proverbs right now. Apply them to your heart. From this one section comes life that only a few achieve if they believe.

I believe as we become more and more intentional with our climbing moves in life, we will begin to understand discernment more and more. As we climb through the years and encounter harder and harder moves, we grow in our capacity to discern our situations. Instead of roping up and jumping on a climb we grow in our ability to discern from the ground what we may encounter. We are able to anticipate and use the knowledge we have grown in to effectively accomplish with discernment the task before us. We won't be wildly trying to crank through that next climb, but knowingly pull through the direct route using the wisdom we have gained from all the years of climbing.

I have had no idea most of my life how I have come into situations that I encounter, but I know this, I have at times been that guy that stood there alone amidst all the people (like Joshua and Caleb) willing to make a decision that goes against everything, but ultimately honors God. Our willingness to go there and be that guy that cries aloud for wisdom enters us into the direct route and keeps us tracking through the ridges and tunnels of life. Many will mock you and tear you down, but if you maintain your upright direction, the Lord will protect you , teach you and guide you . We will discern the right moves whether easy or not. We will have the confidence to make the right choices. We will stand alone, sling our rock, and throw it knowing that God ordained it and will protect it. What are you waiting for? I challenge you to memorize that above section in Proverbs. Keep it close to your heart; for if you do, you will walk a life of integrity and honor. You will understand what righteousness looks like, fairness is, and what is just. God calls it every good path. That good path, the direct route, will fill your heart with wisdom. From that wisdom you will glean knowledge, and a peace will fill you up. Discernment and discretion will come on your life and your understanding will guard you. We must, as Go-To Guys, cry aloud and seek after this. I want it more than anything but I fail constantly to actually implement it in my life. I look to the men ahead of us, the Caleb's and the David's, to help us see clearly what it means to stay consistent. I'm tired of not being more of what we are called to be, than we actually are.

## GO-TO GUY Response

He is a guy who does things in a way that I trust. He is the guy I know would be doing something the way I would or would want to. Maybe I don't know the best route to go on something. Because I know and trust his thinking and processing. I might go to him if I want direction or if I want confirmation on what I am thinking. For me it's a guy who is well thought out. Then he goes and does it with a plan in mind. If his plan is not working he is not locked in. He is able to make adjustments, admit things that are not working, make changes to keep it going, or move on. He is a learner. He is not locked into things that do not work because of his stubborn pride. As a learner he is a listener. There are very few truly new ideas out there. A Go-To Guy knows that listening, gathering, getting thoughts, plans and ideas from others, will keep him from re-inventing the wheel.

–Mike

## THE GO-TO GUY

**2010 EVOLUTION TRAVERSE**

**MT. HAECKEL**
37.1509° N.   118.6609° W

**SECTION THREE**
**THE CRUX**

Being stuck on our ledge could be referred to
as the ledge of life. We have these safe places, but moving
past that headwall in front of us requires
dedication and discernment. We can choose to weather the storm
and chance the outcome, or come back for another day.
The cruxes of life present to us everywhere,
and we have choices to make.

# INTRODUCTION TO SECTION 3

As we approached Mt. Mendel, we dropped down a very steep section of boulders and into a small bowl through a crack system. Most of the time you can figure out where to go. There are various places where you will see where climbers came through and left a piece of protection or a sling wrapped around a rock that they rappelled off of. We dropped off one such piece of protection. It is a little sketchy using others' gear, however, it saves you from giving up precious gear, if you don't have to. As we rapped down with our packs, we were placed on the edge of the ridge right underneath Mt Mendel. We could scoot over and look directly into the Darwin Basin, Lamarck Col. side, or we could look directly out at the evolution basin side. It is one of the places where the wind is swirling around. One side has an updraft; the other blasts you in the face as you look on. We were facing what is known as the golden headwall. There was a small ledge that you could walk between a very protected little ledge and the ridgeline, which looked over toward Lamarck Col. Mind you, the weather was amazing up till this point. It was absolutely sunny with warm temps. But as we descended into this little ledge it was getting very dark. In fact, our ledge was just under the ridgeline on the evolution basin side and we were watching the circling storm system come right towards us. We could hear the thunder and started counting.

Instinct seems to take over when I am in the mountains. We could feel the temperature drop immediately. We were trying to calculate out what the storm was going to do. As we both rested on the ledge, we decided to start putting our clothes on. We had packed good clothes for the ridge and were prepared for bad weather, however, when it started to rain that's when we started to wonder. We could see huge bands of grey streaming down out of the clouds and knew by the temp that it was either going to be some very cold rain or snow. This was where we started to contemplate our trip. We decided to hunker down and put the space blanket on over to protect us to save some heat and provide a little shelter from the rain, as it started to swirl over us. I believe there is a video and a few jokes about the fact that we were using a space blanket at 13,000ft in a lighting/rain/snow storm on top of a mountain ridge. As we joked under the blanket, it started snowing; small flakes, but snowing none-the-less, in July. The realization was upon us that we might need to bail off this climb. If the rock wall in front of us is too wet would we be able to climb it? If we passed it and got caught on Mt. Mendel in a storm could we bail back this way if wet? Is this storm going to pass? It was beginning to be late afternoon and we needed to be on Mt Darwin for the evening bivy. My mind was getting ready, because for Joe, I was going to stay up there and die, if that's what it took to complete our mission. My honest self was saying out loud that if this storm stuck around it could become a very ugly night. And getting off the mountain in a full raging snowstorm/rainstorm was not something I wanted to do. We were in a very good spot to bail down a steep 3,000 ft. gulley. We kept looking over the Darwin Basin side and watching the storm, then looking our direction toward Evolution Basin. It seemed we were surrounded by an ugly storm. We could see lightning and as the storm approached we were struck that this might not be just some easy Sierra summer storm. Most summer storms will push through quickly and return back to normal. In this case we could have waited out the storm. That was not the case with this storm. We decided to bail. Neither of us was happy about it, especially Joe. We were full of so much confidence and will power that it took us quite some time to actually say, "okay, lets get off this mountain."

Being stuck on our ledge could be referred to as the ledge of life. We have these safe places but moving past that headwall in front of us requires dedication and discernment. We can choose to weather the storm and chance the outcome or come back for another day. The cruxes of life present to us everywhere, and we have choices to make. As I watched my best friend make a hard choice to bail that day I realized and watched, as he was able to accept the defeat knowing that ultimately in his mind there was going to be another day on this ridge. This is the difference; this is where the Go-To Guy separates himself from the pack. Amidst the trial or circumstance, he can rise up to meet the circumstance. The defeat actually makes him stronger. Most would accept defeat and probably never go back. The Go-To Guy doesn't see it that way. He sees it as an amazing opportunity to praise God for the experience and to use it to make him stronger. It may take some time, but the attitude changes, they revel in their awesome experience and choose to stay positive, even when the disappointment is lingering. This is where I appreciate the enormity of God and His presence.

Joe and I, although angry and bummed, bailed that day. We succumbed to the storm and discerned that it would be better to come back another day. I feel that the Lord places things in our hearts. This was one of those days because if we had stayed on that ridge that night we might not have had another day.

## NINE
# The Critical Moment

*"I'm Hub McCann. I've fought in two World Wars and countless smaller ones on three continents. I led thousands of men into battle with everything from horses and swords to artillery and tanks. I've seen the headwaters of the Nile, and tribes of natives no white man had ever seen before. I've won and lost a dozen fortunes, KILLED MANY MEN and loved only one woman with a passion a FLEA like you could never begin to understand. That's who I am."*
Hub McCann Secondhand Lions Movie 2003

There are critical moments in every man's life. You know what I mean. These moments where it just seems everything counts, it's all on the line, the seriousness is immeasurable. We have choices during these critical moments and it's how we walk through the moments we have, that shape us into more and more of what the Go-To Guy is. For Joe and I, it wasn't the first time we had been in a precarious situation in the mountains, or in life for that matter. But it was one of those moments where we had to make a difficult decision in order to come back to play another day. We could have stayed up there that day. No doubt…the storm may have blown through that afternoon, but the storm that followed that small afternoon one, would have been two days of misery and put us in a very dangerous place. Coming off evolution in a raging rain and snowstorm would have been a borderline death wish.

The ability to walk through our critical moments is another area I see the Go-To Guy running away from the pack on. Maintaining our identity and authenticity through our critical moments in life really does dictate our direction up to the highest of heights and the lowest of lows. What really intrigues me is that the Go-To Guy uses his moments to define him. He builds strength from the critical times whether good or bad. They mold us into all that we are. We all have many moments in life, but think back to a critical moment in your life where it all hung out on the line. Take a moment to reflect on that moment.

I'm very much captivated by movies. I'm always in awe at how they can build so many parallels and mirror the Bible so closely considering the culture in Hollywood. Look at Gladiator, the movie for instance. We watch as one of the most powerful generals watches his rightful inheritance from the king get stripped from him by the sinister son who squanders everything in his life. We watch as the general gets stripped of everything, his family destroyed, comes chained before his friends who are going to kill him, and gets captured to fight as a gladiator. What is interesting here is that in his critical moment, the gladiator never loses his identity and integrity. He walks straight through the adversity and moments, maintaining what dignity he had left, using all his strength to get to the last critical moment where he stands in front of Rome in the biggest arena and confronts the sinister new king. What an inspiration to stand tall through the most critical time and stand for all that matters! You say, "Hold on Billy, It's only a movie." Okay fine. Lets look at some real life critical moments.

I can think of a man who happens to spend three times a day on his knees overlooking Jerusalem praying. He leads a life trustworthy and void of any corruption or negligence. This man is distinguished above all the administrators and satraps. So much so that the King planned to set him over the whole kingdom. His critical moment comes when he is falsely accused and a trap is set over his life. Now imagine yourself getting thrown into a large rock den. In the back you see massive lions swirling around hungry. Enter the critical moment for Daniel. I would have loved to be a fly on that den wall that day! I can only imagine the courage it took for Daniel to stand there, and call forth in complete trust the protection of the Lord! As Daniel walks through the moment in his life where by a sheer trap, the king is duped into signing a law that would end his friends' life. Can you imagine the king as he runs to the den the next morning and calls out only to find God spared Daniel! Daniel saw forward in blind faith that his moment was under God's control. He walked it out according to his heart, which was in tune with His father.

How does the Go-To Guy embrace the critical moments of life like he does? Where does one get to a place where he can find peace in the decisions it takes to make it through the critical times of our lives? Personally I have never been thrown in a real lions den. I have never been sold into slavery (like Joseph). I never had to make a decision that dictated the fate of a nation. No, what I have are my own circumstances and moments that have shaped my life. Mine are not yours. I believe each moment is ordained by God to bring us into a place that no other person has been or will be the same. Your moments in life are yours. Your moments can be kept secret; you can take them to the grave. What I have seen in men I trust though, is that it's the ability to walk out their critical times and not be afraid to use their moments in life as a backbone of strength and integrity. There are times where our moments are ugly as well! Where we definitely did not walk the direct route. We were way off route. The moment came and we failed. David had a choice when he was watching out a window and saw a beautiful woman bathing. Epic fail, but it brought him to his knees and rounded some rough edges. Now think back to that critical moment in your life you thought of. A moment where everything counted, where you know the outcome could have been life or death. Where you made a great choice, or squandered something. Think back for a moment and vividly recount what happened.

You see many men choose to make agreements with their moments. Here is what I mean. Lets say you are struggling with watching porn, and you are partnering with that sin. You are allowing it into your life. When a critical moment comes and goes, how we respond to that moment is the direction we go. You can choose to partner with that sin and allow it into your life. I have watched many men take a major moment in their life and use it for God's glory regardless of the sin or screw-up. They chose not to make an agreement with the sin. They recognize they are off route and make adjustments to get back on route. You see, the Go-To Guy uses these moments to break off the rough edges. To polish the stone. As men can we all agree we have rough edges? If you don't agree, double back and reread chapter 2. We will wait.

The Go-To Guy uses his moments to shape his life. Are you using the moments in your life to shape yours? As these moments shape us we have a choice to give our utmost or to quit. What I have seen is this innate desire in Go-To Guys to rise above the challenge with a strength that only comes from God. It is inner strength that men are born with but have to polish in order to use effectively. My father in law reminded me of another great critical moment this morning.

> "I would say to the House, as I said to those who have joined this Government: "I have nothing to offer but blood, toil, tears and sweat." We have before us an ordeal of the most grievous kind. We have before us many, many long months of struggle and of suffering. You ask, what is our policy? I can say: It is to wage war, by sea, land and air, with all our might and with all the strength that God can give us; to wage war against a monstrous tyranny, never surpassed in the dark, lamentable catalogue of human crime. That is our policy. You ask, what is our aim? I can answer in one word: It is victory, victory at all costs, victory in spite of all terror, victory, however long and hard the road may be; for without victory, there is no survival. Let that be realized; no survival for the British Empire, no survival for all that the British Empire has stood for, no survival for the urge and impulse of the ages, that mankind will move forward towards its goal. But I take up my task with buoyancy and hope. I feel sure that our cause will not be suffered to fail among men. At this time I feel entitled to claim the aid of all, and I say, "Come then, let us go forward together with our united strength."
> 
> -Winston Churchill May 13, 1940 - First Speech as Prime Minister to the House of Commons.

Churchill had no choice. Back against the wall he had to inspire a nation to rise up past the scary notion that the Nazi's would take them and rule over them. He could have wussed out. He could have given up. Instead he chose to believe. He gave his utmost to see his country succeed. Even to death. He believed, with such a passion, that the Nazi's were wrong, that there was nothing that would stop him in his endeavor to win the war. Whatever it took. He bore a nation, got them to believe, and led them forward. His critical moments were in a series of speeches, but those speeches shaped the destiny of England in the war. Churchill gave his utmost as he knew best. As we grow as men, we have to be willing to stand tall in our moments, trusting that God will deliver us. Daniel trusted in front of those lions, and God sent an angel to shut up the mouths of those lions. That's awesome. Seriously awesome. Men like Daniel inspire me to have more faith; faith that can move mountains. Within that faith, lies the peace that comes from years of moments that have rounded us out, given us courage, and given us eyes to see past the moments and into what God is doing through the moments. You see our moments are giving us ears to listen and eyes to see closer into the heart of God.

There are so many times when I get caught up in the moment and fail to see the bigger picture. It reminds me of the metaphor of the camera. When you look through the viewfinder of a camera what you see is the square box and whatever fits in that box as you look through at your subject. As you move the camera the view changes but you can only see what fits within the boundaries of the viewfinder. We are the viewfinder. We can only see what is in that box as we go through life, but God is the photographer and sees the whole picture. He sees everything. When you pull away from the camera and see the whole picture, then you can understand the scope of God's view as he sees your life. He sees the whole picture and knows the moments that are about to come into your viewfinder. The challenge here is that we as men learn to walk with our viewfinder in expectation of the moments God has for us. We may only see through our viewfinder, but we can trust through faith the bigger picture that God has for us and know that He will walk us through our moments regardless of the storm or the battle. I challenge you to look at your moments as Christ sees your life, not through the viewfinder. Never lose hope. Anticipate what God is going to do in your life. Be on the offensive, not the defensive. If we choose to stand tall through our critical moments, not losing sight of the finish line, we will cross the line and keep going. It never was about the finish line. It was never about the one race or moment. It's about running past the current moment and into the next. I press on toward the goal to win the prize for which God has called me heavenward in Christ Jesus (Philippians 3:14). Press on mighty warriors. As your critical moments happen, press on toward the goal, of the upward call of God.

## GO-TO GUY Response

The ultimate go-to moment in my life came when I was 25 years old. I grew up with my father taking my siblings and I hiking in the Cascade Mountains in Oregon. On this particular hike we ventured up a steep trail just east of Multnomah Falls; it was just my father and me on this day. He had been going through a challenging time as a pastor protecting the church from some significant internal turmoil and testing. He was consistently willing to stand for truth, and shepherd regardless of the cost. Our hike was incredible through the rainforest and winding creeks and waterfalls, but what I will remember most vividly that day is our conversation. I don't recall my exact words but I felt a significant burden to speak into his life encouragement and affirmation, which I did. He looked at me and said, "Thanks David for being my pastor." How is a son to respond to that! At that point in my life the generational baton was passed in an incredible go-to moment. Little would I know that with his death 3 years later that particular moment was an incredible gift from heavenly Father to give specific affirmation and embarkation in my journey as a leader and friend to those God would bring in my life path. I hope to be a part of at least two more of those moments in my life as a father. I know that I am blessed and have a burden to share that blessing with my sons and those around me that have not received that gift from their earthly fathers.

-David

## TEN
# The Ledge

I sat on that ledge in the middle of the Sierra's almost with a satisfaction that can only be described as peace. After rapping down onto this ledge I kept walking over to the small lip that looks over at the Darwin basin side. Weather was swirling around. Patches of sunlight would flicker through the storm cycle but eventually were consumed by grey, cold, moist air. Watching the uncontrollable storm approaching, Joe and I could only hunker down, talk, laugh and wait. I've heard so many stories in the backcountry where rather than wait a storm out and hunker down, climbers set out amidst the storm, get caught up, and some are killed. The backcountry intrigues me with this. It's such a grand and beautiful place. We are so small up there. The ledge is a place where we are in that moment when we feel stuck. When it seems that we can't go up, we can't go down, we seem to be stuck. I want to look at the Go-To Guy and his ledge. Sometimes in life, we are in a situation that we cannot control. We are in a place where we are surrounded. We keep getting pounded in the surf. It seems we will never get to paddle out. Then it seems there is a break in the tide set. That's when we paddle our brains out. We jump off that ledge. We begin to move.

The ledge is a place where we can really feel lost. We can feel the enormity of it all. Life can consume us here. We will make quick decisions. We get on the ledge, and storms seem to surround us. The ledge is lonely. We feel abandoned. It seems our dreams get lost somewhere or we dropped them off the cliff, watching them break apart as they tumble away. How did we get here? As men, once we say those words we jump into high gear to figure it out. We try to make a solution to the problem. We felt alive getting here, but now it's almost scary, as we sit there on the ledge wondering.

What I love about the Go-To Guy is that the ledge is the point that defines him. It is a place where they stand in authority knowing who they are and faithful to the plans and direction God has placed on their life. The Go-To Guy loves the ledge. He almost counts on it. He laughs at the adversity of it; the excitement of it. Watching a storm coming in, swirling around, only invites the Go-To Guy to press in harder. Look at it this way. You are sitting on your ledge. You can climb off your ledge and keep climbing up to the summit, or you can rappel off, dropping into the steep gulley below. Upward represents the summit and the rest of the ridge. Below represents complex down-climbing en-route to the valley floor. What do I do? I like the ledge. It is the place that draws me near to the Lord. You can't go anywhere. You can't hide. You are exposed. You are in the elements. It may seem protective to some extent, but in reality you are standing on a ledge at 13,000ft in a storm. Our response? We worship. Most guys I know do not like being stopped from the goal. Men just go and go regardless of the obstacles. We will fight our way through. We stubbornly reject failure and fumble along striving, striving, striving to get there. Until you hit your ledge. Some men get angry at their ledge. Some men get downright furious at being stuck in a situation that seems to have no way out.

What if we as men saw our ledge as a place to stop and listen? What if we just learned to see the ledge as an awesome place that we landed on as a place of refuge as we hear from the Lord where He wants us to go? Joe and I pressed in that day. We used our time of waiting on that ledge deep in the Sierra's that summer afternoon to press in. We prayed over our beautiful wives, we laughed; we got filled up in what God was doing. We praised him for the lightning and the beautiful ridge. What a chance to be in relationship. I'm here to say that the ridge is a place that at first I had a bad attitude about. "Great, here I am, stuck on this ledge, and it's about to rain. Oh wait, that was a snowflake. Sweet. It's snowing in July." Are you on a ledge right now? What does it look like? Do you feel stuck? I want to encourage you to use your ledge as your place to get connected. Joe has encouraged me every step of my time in this life with him, to get a better perspective of where we are. You may feel left on a ledge or abandoned by God, but what if our perspective was on reflection. Instead of the ledge being lonely, cold, and pointless, what if our ledge was a time to reflect on where we have been? Instead of complaining that we are stuck on a ledge, what if we turned it into a time to look out ahead and reflect on what God is doing? Instead of seeing it as a time where we feel lonely, use it as a time to draw closer. Instead of feeling lost, use it as a time to find our relationship with Him and pursue a deeper connection. You can imagine your time on the ledge as miserable, and do everything you can to get off of it. But think of all that you are giving up by not waiting on the Lord. If we wait on the Lord, He will renew our strength (Isaiah 40:31). I believe the Lord strategically places us men on our ledges in life to teach us and download to us. We have a choice of whether we listen, or we can scatter only to find ourselves on another ledge. I believe as we reflect and listen in those places we will start to understand deeply what God wants to download to us.

For the most part I am as negative as they come. I look at every situation and blatantly will point out the obvious reality. For very positive people, I'm sure it comes across as bothersome. I feel in my heart very positive, but sometimes I just have to say what the truth is, negative or not. Instead of staying positive though, what it does is draw me into negative thinking. As I have walked out my adventure, that has had negative repercussions. The more negative you are, the more negative things you will seek out. You become what you seek after. When I get on the ledge, I can get very negative, but what I have seen in men in my journey, are men who model what it means to stay positive amidst being in a precarious, stuck, position. It doesn't mean we won't get disappointed or angry. But I have watched as those men use their ledges as a time to channel their disappointment and disgust at the situation, into a positive encounter with Christ. They use it as an opportunity to draw deeper in relationship. They are able to reflect and hear God speaking about their place. They are able to lay down the confusion of how they got here, and give it back. What they do effectively is release any feelings they have back to God and instead focus on the good of the situation. Man what a difference this makes in the ability of a mighty man to confront his enemy and walk passionately in the direction called. I believe these ledges are allowed by God for us to garner wisdom, learn from our weaknesses, and grow in passion as men.

Reflection allows the Go-To Guy to look back at where he has been and look out at where he is going. Most Go-To Guys I know see the ledges of life as exciting because they know God is going to show up. They know it. Why? Because time and time again God has been faithful to do it before, and they stand on the promises that they will be fulfilled again. Later on we will talk about looking ahead, but I feel the ledges in our lives offer us a chance, if we are willing, to go deeper into a place that many men just are not willing to go. I feel the Go-To Guy can teach us greatly here how to maintain our identities while standing alone on a ledge in a storm. It is a place that he knows he can, if willing, grow. Many men have lives that are made up of many negative moments. The challenge for all of us is to reflect on where we have been but look ahead with optimism. It doesn't mean dwell on the past. I have seen this too, where many men are just stuck and fixated on everything past tense. Their whole life and every circumstance to come will be dictated by what they already believe. They are living out their past and because of agreements made there, they continue to walk out their lives tied to that past. What I am saying is the Go-To Guy uses all his circumstances in life and reflects on those knowing there are lessons and wisdom to gain from them. BUT, they are already looking ahead, almost relishing the opportunity that is coming next. We have to see our ledges as great times of reflection but also where God wants to show us where we have been and where He is taking us.

You may see the storm coming and the swirling uncertainty, but God sees an opportunity. As men we have to step into these with anticipation of what God is going to do. The Go-To Guy understands this tool well and keeps it at ready access in his tool belt. We have to anticipate what God is doing and be ready for every chance we get to gain wisdom. As we step closer in that relationship and grow in our identities, the Lord is able to walk us down paths that we are now ready for. As we continually position ourselves before the Lord, we can be ready for all that He has and all He is going to do. I had peace that day on that ledge with Joe. A peace that only comes because we knew God was speaking. As reflection happens you will begin to see God open the path and the direction. The ledge seems to be more inviting than catastrophic. I feel like our ledges were designed to help us sharpen up, bring it back to Him, and get focused. As we refocus our eyes on Him, He shows us more than we can imagine. He moves us into our next step. We can get off our ledge.

## GO-TO GUY Response

Romans 6 is a passage I have been studying and working through and it has impacted me immensely. He (Paul) tells us that everybody is a slave to something; either a slave to sin or a slave of God. We once were enslaved by sin and associated in a body of death. But because of Christ's resurrection and of course His grace, we are now alive in Him and dead to sin. He was a man that was sold out to Christ and the lived to see people come to Christ while maintaining his testimony in the way he spoke, acted, and responded to trials. This, in my opinion, is a great example of a "Go-to guy."

Again I believe I can associate many men as "Go-to guys" for me as I have hit different stages in life. They, in their own unique ways, have left lasting impressions on me in family, church, evangelism, work, etc.

–Mark

## ELEVEN
# The Crux

I remember back to my very first climb outside. It was at the basalt black cliffs outside of Boise, Idaho. My closest buddies and I were visiting the climbing shop and looking at gear. We started looking at what to buy, the bare necessities to get by outside. I remember vividly when we made our first trip out to the Black Cliffs. We practically ran up that steep trail to the tall cliff section. We sat there looking up, mesmerized by the guys we were watching. All we had was our harnesses, shoes, chalk bags, and one locking carabiner each (enough gear for us poor high school kids). I think we were hoping to bum a belay or two from whoever was out there. Sure enough they called over to us and asked if we wanted to rope up. Oh man…we jumped on that warm rock that day with reckless abandon. I was set up on a top rope on a route called Beta Junkies (5.10c), my very first outdoor route, ever. I think they were laughing at us because we had brand new shoes and gear. Not even dirty. I bolted up that thing and as I approached the top I was taught a very quick lesson. I had no idea what a crux even was. So there I was, 75ft up, jammed into the base of a rock that protrudes straight out over my head, somewhat overhung. I sat there going, "How in the world do you get over this?" I will admit I did hang for a minute or two. However, one of the guys below, surprised I had made it that far no doubt, shouted out to me exactly what I needed to do to make the moves over the overhang. Move by move, I went somewhat over that protruding rock. After progressing through the crux that day, I was overcome with such an amazing exhilaration! It was my first crux and definitely not my last. The crux is that moment where we have to do the hardest part of the climb. No doubt, moving over the crux that day brought me into a new understanding of the crux and the ability to gain wisdom and understanding to move past those difficult moments on our climbs in life.

I returned to the ground that day a different person. I was so pumped up! My arms were so pumped that I could barely move my muscles. But from that day on I spent almost every weekend of the rest of my high school days ripping through every route in that place. As we moved from one accomplishment to the next, we were gaining in our ability to move past the cruxes of each climb. The cruxes in life can be difficult. They can break a man. They can bring us to new heights. Climbers spend years working on projects, learning all the moves of specific climbs. You see, for years after that, I would have friends come out to climb at those black cliffs.

They would get up that to that same point where that overhang is and make a move to get over. But the moves they took were the wrong ones and it led them to a place where they got stuck. You would see them come flying off the rock and swing down a few feet. Then you would here the inevitable, "How the crap do you get over this part?!" As you scream up to them that they went the wrong way and need to grab the lie-back hold up left, the light comes on and they realize the direct route over the crux. They jump back on route, crank over the crux section and get to the top. I think we can learn a lot from the Go-To Guy here. I needed the help from those guys way back in high school to make it over the crux. It wasn't easy. It took everything I had. But after getting the beta I needed, I was able to accomplish it. How vital it is to have the right information as we maneuver the cruxes of life!

In the mountains near Mt Charleston, in the Compton Cave, is an amazing overhung section of sport climbing outside of Las Vegas, Nevada. I had some specific routes picked out that I wanted to accomplish. Over and over again I would start at the bottom and lead my way through the route into the overhung section, and right at the crux I would make this one move and never be able to pull through the section. I would take a good 30ft whipper and swing around upside down as I flew through the air. The problem here is that if you come off on the crux it is very hard to get back on route because you are basically hanging upside down. Over and over for days I would keep striving. My climbing partner kept saying what if you tried using a lie-back and moved through using a right pull? I would scream back, "It'll never work!" Away I went, I would climb super fast until I got to the crux, and then pop off right as I did the move I thought would get me past the section. On the last day we were supposed to be there I finally decided to try my climbing partner's advice. Sure enough when I got to the crux, I moved through it like I had done this climb with my eyes closed. It was so easy! Striving to do it my way was hindering me from seeing the way. It was blinding me from what my climbing buddy was showing me. I wasn't willing to listen. I thought I could tackle it on my own strength and in my own pride.

The crux is a decision time. It usually requires of us a decision to be made, wherein we move a direction, at the hardest point. I believe this is a major point in men finding breakthrough from the cruxes of life. Many men really strive in their choices. What does that mean you ask? You know exactly what I'm talking about. We men are stubborn. I'm definitely high on the stubborn list. My wife has no doubt watched me strive through many choices and push through my angst as I try to just get something done. I always push to get things done fast. It's in my nature. When things hold me up, I can get this crazy look in my eye and just snap and start going crazy. I have to finish and accomplish what I had set out to do no matter what. It could be something as stupid as mowing the lawn, or just getting groceries. We men just will give everything we have to finish the job. It could be we have somewhere to be and started a project, but have to finish the project, before we could ever leave. I'm sure you have some examples of your own. Whatever it is, we men are always pushing through something and sometimes striving in our choices.

What I'm getting at here is that striving can lead to wrong choices as we meander through the cruxes in our lives. Pride can take many forms, but regardless, it will poke its head out here and lead us into choices we really never meant to make in the first place. As men we must be willing to see the crux as the hardest point but use our abilities as men of God to walk out the route God is leading us into and encouraging us past. There may be ledges and cruxes, no doubt designed to draw us closer into the heart of God, but we have a choice in those places. We can choose to continue on in our prideful responses, push through our problems and stress in strife. We can decide to walk the wrong line; it's your choice. You see, when you feel tempted to sin, you have a choice.

Climbing is a great parallel, but lets get right to it. The devil knows how we as men are hardwired. He knows your weaknesses. He looks to keep you in a place that keeps you from moving past your crux or your ledge. He spends every second of his worthless existence trying to keep you from making it past those choices. As we make agreements with sin and choices that keep us from pushing past our crux, we come to the meat and root of the issue. We must, as men, enable ourselves to make choices worthy of our Savior. You could be in a place right now where you are struggling with something. That something, whether addiction or an affair, or something you struggle with, is a crux. I have found in my own life that I am astounded how I will make a choice to agree with sin basically almost without my own doing. I literally seconds later will say to myself, "what are you doing?" As the sin gets stronger, it becomes the front lines in a man's battle with sin. It's not about winning every battle. We are all sinners and will sin at some point, but living from a place that protects how we make decisions and how we respond in the face of opposition will dictate future battles and ultimately future cruxes you may face.

Look, we have all been in that place where we are faced with a choice. You could be alone and about to look at porn, or maybe alone with your girlfriend crossing a line you shouldn't, maybe you are cheating on your wife, or maybe you are cheating your business partner; whatever your circumstance, the crux is the same. You have a choice. In that one moment you have a choice that dictates your direction. You can choose to partner with the sin (pride, selfishness, addiction….) and continue in it. The immediate gratification will be there, a useful tool the devil uses as the addiction to it increases, but it fades usually to guilt, shame, and self-condemnation. Then as we continue on in the agreements we have made with those sins, we find ourselves appalled at the place we are at. For me, it is usually the point where I am completely fed up with where I am because in my heart I know I am down the wrong road.

The other side of the choice is the forward progress we make when we move past our crux. As climbers know, there is a sweet gratification when we move past a problem or crux we have been working on. The accomplishment is fulfilling and sweet. As we move into a place of purity in our lives as men we begin to live from the freedom and excitement of living a life that is clean and pure. This is not simple. It requires of us ears to listen, relationship with others, and the ability to step closer in our relationship with Christ. The Go-To Guy, through years of cruxes and ledges, begins to ask the Holy Spirit to change his heart. We let go of the agreements we have made. We walk in purity. The cruxes of life do not necessarily get easier as we go along, but like climbing, each crux before prepares you and teaches you something new that can be used for future battles. These are weapons in your quiver to be pulled when you face another crux. You see, when we equip ourselves through our experiences, and live from our identities, we can go through and over anything!

"I can do all things through Christ who strengthens me!! (Philippians 4:13)" I have no doubt the hardest climb is still coming, but as men we have to make choices that positively influence our walk in Christ and that positively affect the direction He has for us in this life. Continue climbing, continue going after the cruxes in your life. Don't give up regardless of your situation. Continue to believe that He has done a good work in you.

> Joshua 1:9, " *Have I not commanded you? Be strong and courageous. Do not be terrified; do not be discouraged, for the Lord your God will be with you wherever you go."*

What are you waiting for? The crux you face is nothing for you. You were designed for the adventure you are on! Your journey is amazing. Live it. Get to it. Conquer you crux.

## GO-TO GUY Response

*"The guy that is there for you no matter what. The guy who knows your faults yet doesn't get hung up on them. The guy that has your back no matter what. The guy that prays with you. The guys that introduces you to people and ideas that change the coarse of your life. The guy that has the holy spirit alive and well within him."*
-Ryan

## TWELVE
# Amidst the Trial

As a cross-country runner, we would train and train for every imaginable and unimaginable circumstance that arises during a race. My years in high school and college taught me many lessons about racing and training for big races. In races you gain wisdom about race strategy, weather and altitude, nervousness, pack running, terrain, racing tactics, and mentally staying composed. Through the years racing you gain a practical knowledge and lessons that train you. Through every circumstance, we trained to meet those circumstances to win the race as a team and do the best as individuals that we could. How do we carry this mentality into our daily lives so that we can rise up amidst the trial and run the race before us? I believe this is the quintessential piece embedded in the Go-To Guy that pushes that man to do things unimaginable. It enables Him to go places never gone before. It accomplishes through Him the identity placed in him, to be all that he can be. All the critical moments, all the ledges, all the cruxes, they are just that. They are circumstances in life that unless we push past, can hold us back, potentially causing us to get lost.

My challenge here to you, as we pursue what it means to be Go-To Guys, is that we have to be overcomers. In cross-country there is usually a lead pack till about the latter half of the race, when everyone begins to get strung out over the racecourse. This is where the Go-To Guy separates himself from the pack, overcomes the circumstance, and rises above to win the race. We have to train ourselves to allow the Lord to overcome us, so we can be overcomers. We need the breakthrough in our lives, seen or unseen, to grow in wisdom so we can be prepared to push past, and rise above the trial. As we live in our trials, and you know what I'm talking about; as you live and walk out that crux or ledge going on right now in your life, are you prepared to meet it head on, laugh at the adversity, and overcome it?

What trial are you in right now? What ledge or crux are you standing on? Take a moment to think about it. Just close your eyes and think about it for a second. Identify the place you are struggling with right now. By now I'm sure you have thought about a way out. I'm always directing my wife in a way to solve her problems; the classic guy solution to everything right? What I fail to see with her is that she needs me to hear her, not necessarily solve it for her. As I have come to understand this I can stand with her, not dictate to her the next move. As we stand together, we can nail to the cross the situation and move forward. My typical response to her though is to immediately blurt out some solution. To establish the ground that I'm some supreme manly answer to all her problems! As I have grown to understand my wife and my role as a husband, I can now see my wife in a different light and try my best to understand her, and if asked, help her walk through a trial or circumstance. Where I'm going with all this is that the Go-To Guy uses his past victories to walk into the present fight and overcome it. It takes a calculated response that is not based on adrenaline or to fill a need. Our responses become a direct reflection of the years of wisdom and sacrifice, and strength of will over our minds and bodies to make sound decisions. It embodies years of surrendering and trusting. In turn we begin to respond to circumstances rationally.

Here's a good way to look at it. When you begin to shoot a handgun, you are taught to slowly learn how to draw your weapon, aim it, and slowly pull the trigger. By doing this painfully slow, you are learning the right way to draw your weapon, aim it, and squarely and smoothly shoot at the target. You are training yourself to do it right every time, by repetition. As your abilities grow to hit the target, you can slowly begin to speed up your approach. As I have seen with the best shooters, they have years of painstaking practice to perfect the art of shooting, but with a speed that is unparalleled. They train themselves to go faster and faster but rely on the years of perfection with their training. Since they were willing to learn to shoot right, they now can go faster because their default is precise shooting. You never start out shooting by going as fast as you can! As we see men in high stress situations making sound decisions, we can see they have years of practice in circumstances where they learn over to time to make wise and sound choices. Instead of shooting wildly all over the place and sometimes hitting the target, these men hit the target every time because they choose to have control over their situations. A commonality with Go-To Guys is that they can make very sound decisions amidst stressful situations.

Looking at Saul in 1st Samuel Chapter 13, we see two men make decisions and the consequences of those decisions. Saul was King and had just formed Israel's first standing army. Jonathan, his son, was the leader of one of those first armies. Jonathan, a mighty military leader full of integrity, initiated an attack on a small portion of Philistines stationed in Geba with his men. This alerted the Philistines to garner their resources and prepare for battle with the Israelites. Saul was in Gilgal, and having heard of the attack on the Philistines, sounded the trumpets throughout Israel. At this, the Israelites heard that Saul had attacked the Philistines. We begin to see Saul's heart here in this situation. On the one hand Jonathan was listening to what God wanted, on the other hand we see his father taking credit for something Jonathan did; we begin to see his insecurities as King. Saul gathers the Israelites in Gilgal to prepare for battle. The Israelites see the massive army being gathered against them and begin to hide in fear. Jonathan had initiated the attack boldly going with his belief that God was going before them. Saul, sitting in Gilgal was told by Samuel to wait until He got there, so Samuel could prepare the sacrifice and prepare Israel spiritually for battle. Saul in haste, adrenaline pumping because of fear of the Philistines and the massive army, fear of losing and time of the essence, decides to offer up an offering. Out of fear or panic, and clearly not knowing what to do in the face of the impending crisis, Saul gives the burnt offering. An hour later Samuel arrives and says, "What have you done?" (1 Sam 13:11) Saul goes out to greet Samuel clearly knowing he had blown it by not trusting and waiting on the Lord. He hastily took it upon himself in the heat of the moment to provide an answer to the circumstance at hand.

People scattering from him, the Philistines camped nearby, Samuel not there yet, so Saul decides to take it upon himself to carry the Israelites. Amidst the trial, Saul sinned against the Lord. Unlike Jonathan, who called upon the Lord and listened, Saul presented an answer to the crisis that showed his insecurities and lack of trust in the Lord. His decision was not based on surrender and trust, wisdom and past victories. Instead it was a decision based on insecurity and pride, ruled by his feelings and self-image. The Go-To Guy bases his decisions on being overcome by Him, so that he can be open and transparent, surrendering every aspect of his life. By doing this his decisions become not his own, but of Christ. As we continue to continually throw our trust back to God, we become overcomers. Our decisions in the trials reflect God's heart. He gives us the answers; he provides us the hope and the determination to overcome anything. We can overcome regardless of the thirty thousand men and chariots just over the hill. Are you willing to listen and surrender, to be overcome by Him?

If we fast-forward to the First World War, in the exact same place as Jonathon, a place called Micmash in Palestine, was one of General Allenby's British Brigades. Under the dim light of a candle a brigade major was searching fervently for a name in his Bible. This particular brigade major had received orders to attack and overtake a village nestled on a rocky prominence at the far end of a deep valley. It was called Micmash and this Brigade Major felt it oddly familiar.

As he read through 1 Samuel 13 he came across where Saul and Jonathan were camped. It reads, 'Saul and his son Jonathan and the men with them were staying in Gibeah in Benjamin, while the Philistines camped at Micmash. As he read further, 'On each side of the pass that Jonathon intended to cross to reach the Philistine outpost was a cliff; One was called Bozez, and the other Seneh. One cliff stood to the north toward Micmash, the other to the south toward Geba (1 Samuel 14:4-5). The Major continued reading, 'Jonathan climbed up, using his hands and feet, with his armor-bearer right behind him. The Philistines fell before Jonathan, and his armor-bearer followed and killed behind him. In that first attack Jonathan and his armor-bearer killed some twenty men in an area of about half an acre. Then panic struck the whole army-those in the camp and field, and those in the outposts and raiding parties-and the ground shook. It was panic sent by God.' The Major kept reading and saw how the whole Philistine army melted away in all directions and in their panic were even fighting themselves! Saul attacked with his whole force and defeated them.

After reading this, the Brigade Major thought to himself that this passage in Micmash must still exist through Bozez and Seneh (the two rock prominences) as well as the half acre of land. He mustered his commander and after reading through the verses once more, they sent patrols to find this place. The patrols found a small group of Turks guarding a pass with two jagged prominences (Bozez and Seneh). Upon finding the half acre of land, one company was sent through the pass, overpowering the small group of Turks. The cliffs were quickly overtaken and the company was soon standing at the ready on the half acre of land. Much like how the Philistines awoke in confusion, the Turks awoke and started running in every direction, obviously feeling surrounded by Allenby's army. As the story goes they were all captured or killed. Allenby's army was successful in defeating the Turks on the same ground, using the same tactics that Saul and Jonathan did!

-Werner Keller, A Remarkable Occurrence, Extract from "The Bible as History, A Confirmation of the Book of Books" (1956)

Sitting on my ledge on Evolution Traverse was more of a metaphor for things in my life than it was a major decision. What it represents though is how the Go-To Guy is resilient in standing firm for what is in his heart; for what is placed in his heart. We see Jonathan be an overcomer as he followed his heart after God's heart. We watch thousands of years later as a Brigade major in the British army follows his heart after he recognized a name in the Bible and how it led him to defeat the Turks in the same place as Jonathan defeated the Philistines. Let's as men, decipher through our circumstances on our ledges and cruxes with discernment and stand on our past victories. We have amazing Godly men who have gone before us and shown us by example how to surrender and be overcome in their walks with God. As we do this it will lead us to train how to be effective and on target when we shoot. We will not be wildly shooting from the hip, but directly on target. It will teach us how to push past the trials and to step above the circumstances that happen in life. Saul chose to trust himself and act out of haste. We have a choice. When you come to your choice amidst the trial, seek after being overcome in your heart by the Lord. "He will never fail you nor forsake you." Stand on the past victories and declare over your life that because of the cross you are an overcomer. Seek to be a man after God's own heart. As we do this we will do the unimaginable. We will defeat the impossible and walk right past it. A good friend of mine wrote me once saying, "It is easier said than done, but keeping our hearts and minds on Him we are never led astray." Well said, Go-To Guy. I have no doubt that the Go-To Guys in heaven would agree…

## GO-TO GUY Response

That's a tough question... But I would say seeing the big picture of life and the perspective that God is walking with us no matter how bad it gets. It's always easier said than done, but keeping our hearts and minds on him we are never lead astray. I think it is a life long surrendering and trusting process -Tyler

I think for some guys it is a one-time thing, but it may not necessarily be a good thing. For instance, a boy being bullied who finally cracks and kicks the other guys' butt, that may or may not work, and if it does it is not a strategy to be implemented on every similar occasion. This could be called the immature guy. The mature guy is a guy who has taken small steps all along the way accruing experiences so that the current trial, though a challenge, can be overcome not by pure adrenaline but through wisdom, diplomacy, and strength of the will and body. The catalyst really is how bad do you want it? That is the launch, the impetus, but the success is taking the victories of the past and applying them to the present.

-Jason

## THE GO-TO GUY

**2010 EVOLUTION TRAVERSE**

**MT. HUXLEY**
37.1362° N.   118.6828° W

**SECTION FOUR**
**THE DESCENT**

*The Go-To Guy lives his journey, all the while using his experiences to strengthen, encourage, and empower others to see Christ and their potential. This fundamental truth is what keeps him going. The Go-To Guy lives his journey whether winning or in defeat. He lives from his heart. He embraces his life and takes it stride for stride.*

# INTRODUCTION TO SECTION 4

When we bailed, we found a dirty, nasty old sling wrapped around a chockstone. Most would have left their own gear and rapped off of that, however, we tested the sling, felt confident it would hold, and proceeded to rappel off of it. I can honestly say that was a bit of a sketchy sling we rapped off. As I watched the headwall get smaller as I descended from it, I was sad to be giving up, seemingly so easy. We were presented with a very steep gully to make our way through to get down to the John Muir Trail in the Evolution Basin. There were snow patches up high, and as we made our way down through some very loose rock sections, we talked. I count these moments with Joe as some of my most cherished times. We talk about everything from our wives to work, to our dreams and goals. He inspires me, encourages me, and walks it out with me; all the while bailing from a climb that we were both so passionate about accomplishing. The importance of the journey could not be more understated here.

The Go-To Guy lives his journey, all the while using his experiences to strengthen, encourage, and empower others to see Christ and their potential. This fundamental truth is what keeps him going. The Go-To Guy lives his journey whether winning or in defeat. He lives from his heart. He embraces his life and takes it stride for stride. Our descent that day was actually such a blast. I was inspired by my friend to dig deeper into me; to trust my heart and live out my dreams. We passed amazing water holes and into a beautiful steep meadow section with Evolution Lake right in front of us. The sun popped out underneath the storm clouds as it was setting. It was one of the most beautiful evenings I have ever seen. If I had bailed just for that, it would have been worth it. The entire evolution basin was filled with an intense afterglow.

We finally hit the trail pretty tired. We knew we had a couple of miles to go to get to our tent! We headed along the lake and then proceeded down the hill a bit until we reached the hard to find trailhead for the Darwin Bench. At this point we were both rather delirious and started acting funny and stupid. We also got testy with each other. As we get tired we start barking at each other. Another thing I love about the Go-To Guy is that they love unconditionally. What a mirror of Christ's love. No matter the circumstance or how tired, they still keep trudging up that steep trail to reach the destination. We reached the Darwin Bench only to watch an incredible sunset over the Sierra's. We stood there at the tent wasted, tired, laughing, realizing that even though we bailed, we accomplished something awesome. We may have our goals, but God has his lessons. We slept hard that night after a warm meal and laughing our heads off about stupid stuff.

We awoke the next morning to a cold bitter day. It was in every way confirmation that God knew we needed to get off that mountain. As we packed up and hiked toward the Lamarck Col we watched the ridge up above. It was ugly. We would have been blown, or snowed off that mountain the night before and into the next day. It was ugly. As we neared the end of the Darwin Basin before heading up to the Col the floodgates opened and it started hailing and pouring. We ran for cover, which looked more like a pile of rocks with a small hiding place. We created a makeshift cover and cooked some hot food as we watched it pour down rain. It was incredible. If we had been on that ridge in that downpour we would have been screwed. We just started laughing at the hilarity of the event. It was forecasted for sunny blue skies and here we are in some raging massive classic Sierra storm. Awesome! I do believe that Joe mentioned that his hot freeze-dried meal that day was better than sex. He was just going crazy with how good it tasted in that moment.

We trudged up to the Col in cloudy windy weather. As we crested over and said goodbye to Evolution Traverse, we watched as clouds began covering and swirling around it. Our hike out ended up being rather comical. At this point we were making this epic and it got even rainier. As we headed down the steep section toward the car, it was dumping rain. We were tired and frustrated at the top and as we came down the mountain Joe mentioned we just need to enjoy our time. This was better than anything in SOCAL right? We could be stuck on the freeway, or getting yelled at by our boss. Instead we were investing into our dreams. We were laughing our way through another epic adventure. As we looked for another campsite on the way down, we stopped and put mosquito repellant on. The rain was making the crazy Sierra critters come out. Well, unbeknownst to me, I had left the repellant at the last stop on the ridge, so that when we got to a camp spot we liked, we were getting eaten alive. We only had a tent rain fly, so we had to build up dirt around the fly that night to keep the mosquitoes out. As we watched the lightning storm rip across the ridge above us, we laughed and howled as we killed mosquito after mosquito that somehow managed to get in there. We figured at one point they were just burrowing through the dirt. There was a duct tape hot chocolate incident and many more before we got to the car.

We proceeded to drive straight into Bishop and eat the biggest breakfast we could get. We ended the trip at Kios Hotsprings and hung out contemplating our journey. By no means did this mean we would not be coming back. In fact, our resolve was being strengthened. We were already planning what we would and wouldn't do for round two. We were buddies living the dream. Walking the walk. Encouraging each other and challenging each other. The Go-To Guys.

## THIRTEEN
# Positive Defeat

Climbers always get this interesting viewpoint as you rappel off certain points in climbing. It's almost like a runner's high. There is a satisfaction with knowing what you accomplished. As you rap off of a climb, you have this inner peace of what was just overcome. I always love to stop and look out behind me while I'm climbing. It's interesting that even in defeat that day on evolution, I watched that chockstone get smaller and smaller as I rapped down with a sense of excitement. I could see the clouds up above, swirling around, like the eye of a storm. I had no idea what that crazy canyon had for us as we dropped into it on our descent. The cruxes we face can change our direction but it cannot change our destination and destiny. Like I said before, the Go-To Guy is living the journey. Even though we bailed from evolution that day, the journey continued.

Positive defeat can define your attitude as you weather the storms in life. The failure to accomplish what you set out to do does not change who you are or define your identity. It only strengthens your resolve. Go-To Guys know this in their hearts and lead from the ability to pick up the slack, move past the hard stuff, and continue on. Where the difference lies is in the attitude. They remain positive. They recover from their fall and continue to trust in the promises instilled in their hearts. Their ability to trust the Lord and not the outside negative influences defines them. I've always enjoyed the descent from a climbing trip because it causes us to reflect and contemplate what was just accomplished or not accomplished. Many men take defeat from a situation and let it own them. I believe we must learn to live out bailing from a climb or a defeat as positive progress in our lives!

Positive defeat may be a new term for some of you but look past the words and think about this: positive defeat is the ability to respond to a defeat or a failure in a way that positively impacts your journey. It is a choice that you have in any circumstance. As we look at what the Go-To Guy models for us we can see this ability to look at simple defeats and absolutely absurd failures as a teaching tool. The main emphasis here is that through a man's life we walk out many different circumstances that build on each other. If we spend our whole life building failure and defeat on top of each other, all you have is a massive mountain of defeats. How on earth do you overcome that? Thankfully we have a model that we have seen in men since the Bible. Whether you have a mountain of failures, like I have built, or a small mound of defeats, we can choose to have an attitude that fosters the positive not the negative. We must have a platform to stand on built from past experiences. A Go-to response, if you will, for the hard times. It doesn't mean you always have the perfect response for every situation, but as we work on it, it becomes a part of us. Our attitude gradually changes to that which we believe for and trust in. Our renewed attitude strengthens us to have hope for the next adventure, building a resolve to learn how to push past areas that were once roadblocks. Our attitude encourages a recovery from failures based on encouragement, hope, trust, and belief. If we negatively respond to our circumstances we begin to believe in the discouragement, disbelief and hopelessness that we trust in. I believe that the Go-To Guy, even in defeat, stays aligned to what he believes inside, the promises given to us by the Lord.

Back when I was training at the US Olympic training center in Chula Vista, Jim Bauman was a sports psychologist there that was looking at the way U.S. Navy SEALS were training and what was the edge required of them to conquer the hardest situations possible. They were looking at ideas and modalities that the Navy was using to train men to be the smartest, toughest, fighters on earth. They were looking to see if there were any ideas they could apply towards athletes looking not only to make an Olympic team, but also getting Olympic medals. Along with the obvious physical attributes, what were they doing psychologically to push through the hardest moments? You see, after you train as an athlete for 10-15 years, it's not about your physical ability as much as it is your mental ability. The mental edge is what the SEALS have. They wanted to see if there were some ideas they could apply toward Olympic hopefuls.

How do we continue to mentally train ourselves to be the Go-To Guys God designed us to be? You might be saying right now, "I'm not a Navy SEAL, or an Olympic athlete." Yep, I get that. I believe that every guy can be a Go-To Guy though. Whether you believe you are one or dream about it. I believe you can walk out all that God has for you in your identity. Listen to what I'm about to say. You can walk out your identity. I was learning from Joe that day on the mountain. He was teaching me, encouraging me to see my own potential and what I was capable of accomplishing. It had nothing to do with our trip on Evolution Traverse. God had ordained that moment for us to encourage each other, raise each other up, get pumped for what we have in life, and positively look forward to the future. The adventure is the journey. The adventure was the crazy training we did trying to out do each other before Evolution. The journey was in building a climbing wall on the side of my house. There was a goal (completing Evolution Traverse) but we were living from our hearts.

# POSITIVE DEFEAT

*"There are three primary domains that we can learn about from this relationship with the SEALs," said Bauman. "All three involve genetic talent, physical (hardware) and mental (software), as well as an environment that will encourage the predisposition to be great." (quoting Jim Bauman, Story Number: NNS071218-15Release Date: 12/18/2007 2:09:00 PM, By Mass Communication Specialist 2nd Class (AW/NAC) Kevin Beauchamp, Naval Warfare Center Public Affairs)*

'An environment that will encourage greatness'. I believe the Go-To Guy learns to achieve greatness by encouraging others to push through their limits and to develop skills that promote them further into their dreams, identities, and journey with the Lord. I was learning from Joe that day what positive defeat looked like. There are the obvious disappointments that come with defeat and failure, but Joe was showing me a side that I have always pushed aside in favor for a negative view. He was showing me that we could change our perspective right then. Instead of spending the next 6 hours of bailing from the climb in disappointment he chose to encourage me.

Not only does positive defeat affect your attitude but I also believe positive defeat defines your identity. You become what you believe. As our bubble gets popped or we have a setback, we can choose right then and there with our attitude to "check it-and change it", as my wife and I often do with each other. As your attitude changes it changes your identity as well. You see, instead of believing in the defeat or failure, you are choosing to push past, effectively changing your identity. You now believe in the positive side of the situation instead of the side that brings you down. Your identity begins to stand on the trust and belief that although you did not accomplish this goal, the hope remains, you are not defeated, and you are free to walk in thankfulness and grace for the moment. The inherent responses you had toward defeat changes to reflect your heart and attitude. As your identity is pointed back toward the cross, it begins to reflect what's inside. Joe was encouraging greatness in me before Evolution, during Evolution, and after Evolution. As we learn to respond as positive men, we freely encourage others in their journey. We are all walking out our lives, but we can learn a lot from the Go-To Guys out there.

I would venture to say that if we met up with Peter from the Bible for some coffee and asked him if he ever thought he would deny Jesus three times, he would probably say no. But he did. A few days after denying Jesus, he picks up the pieces and is preaching a sermon to thousands after Christ's death. Wow. Talk about positive defeat. Peter is a true example of a man who overcame his failures. What is amazing is how Peter, exudes the grace bestowed on him by Christ, and later in his ministry leads the church by that same grace to raise the dead and heal the sick. I believe Peter was a walking example of how we can grow through our failures. He says later in his ministry, "But grow in grace, and in the knowledge of our Lord and Savior Jesus Christ." (2 Pt. 3:18) This guy tested Christ, denied Him, and failed to keep his eyes on Jesus causing him to sink. We all have our failures, however Peter, was not allowing his failures to define his life. This guy saw rebound with a perspective that most of us could learn from. This journey that we are all on would only be complete if we fail sometimes. Congratulations, you are normal. I think it was so great that Peter was a fisherman. Isn't it great how Peter falls back on what he does best when he failed the worst? He went back to fishing. Christ shows up after everything Peter went through and restores Him. Peter stood back up, willing to walk out his journey, willing to let go of his past. Peter being the overcomer, walked out the rest of his journey with the grace and authority bestowed on him because he understood positive defeat.

Another close friend of mine shared this recently with me.

> *The human temptation is always to want to tell God the story He should tell with our lives. Last year I was preparing for the summer Olympics in London. Years earlier I had left my previous coach and started an innovative training method*

that I dubbed, "faith-based coaching," by which I applied everything I that I learned from the Bible and ultimately woke up and asked God what I should do for my training each day. I was completely dependent on Him and hearing his voice. In my mind I could see the painting that God was painting. I had risked my entire career in pursuit of Him and now he was going to honor that in front of millions. I had been on various TV shows and done more interviews then I could count talking about my unique approach to training and how much I loved God. I was sure that like Eric Liddel, when the marathon day came, God would "honor those who honor Him."

The race started and I took off with the early leaders, however my breathing felt labored and I felt like I was running a 3-mile race, not a 26.2-mile race. I'd had this feeling before so I coached myself through it by encouraging myself, 'this is just a bad patch, just ride it out you will start feeling better soon.' I hung on until about 6 miles when I noticed a grabbing in my right hamstring. Again I flooded my mind with memories of what God had done in previous marathons when my calves got tight very early. The lead group was now getting away from me and the negative thoughts continued to flood in but I battled them off thinking, 'God will do a miracle. They will come back. Just get through this mile. You will start feeling better soon." In actuality I was not feeling better.

*My hamstring continued to get tighter and tighter and I began to limp. No matter how positive my thought life and no matter how much I wanted it or believed, my circumstances did not change. This was not the story that I thought was being painted. This is not what the world was supposed to see, a Christian suffering. Or maybe it is exactly what the world was supposed to see. A Christian suffering. A Christian who's dreams are being shattered before his eyes yet still has something in him that is he can never lose. A hope and a joy that cannot be taken. A Christian that though he loses in the worlds eyes, he never really loses because he already has something far greater than a gold medal. I remember one of the last thoughts that I had that day as I came to a walk and dropped out of my first ever race was, "I'd rather lose with God, than win without him." He truly is our true dream, our true destiny. All our other dreams are minor in comparison. He is enough and so is His grace. Following Him doesn't mean we will always win and be prosperous but if we realize it, it does mean we have already won the most important race of our lives.*

 *Today, I am still in pursuit of the vision God gave me 17 years ago. Even though I still get bummed out and discouraged when injuries and bad races come my way I am learning to get up even quicker and it takes a lot more to take my hope as I have learned to realize that with God*

> *you can't lose. I am still going after God and using my "faith-based" approach to training. I am still making mistakes along the way but getting better at laughing at them. I am getting to the point in my running career where I can pursue breakthrough in running yet still be content with the breakthrough God has given me as I continue to master the technique of falling forward. –Ryan Hall*

Ryan is right; failing forward must be our pursuit. Go-To Guys, through practice, can keep the big picture. The pictures change as we walk through different phases in our lives, but we can maintain a larger picture that guides us. I believe we can learn from that. We must continually look up at the cross, much like that chockstone on Evolution and trust that it will hold us as we rappel down the defeats and failures in life. As we do this, our core faith and trust comes alive. We learn to see the defeats and failures as a positive part of our journey. Whether you are on the biggest stage or the smallest, our focus must be on the fact that we have already won. Christ has already won. I want to encourage you to push into fostering a positive atmosphere in all that you do. As we work on our responses in the hard times, we are building, teaching, and modeling a Go-To Guy response. As we do this, Christ wants to mold us like clay and make us into the likeness of Him. Laying our attitudes down and trusting the Lord's will is paramount as we venture through life. Whether you are standing on top of Mt Everest, just got laid off, waiting in line for groceries, or on the starting line for the Olympics, begin to choose thankfulness over negativity. Learn to encourage others around you to greatness. Begin to build your amazing life experiences, whether defeats or wins, as positive steps in your journey.

## *GO-TO GUY Response*

*I know that there are at least 2 guys (maybe 3) who would take out a second mortgage on their house for me if I REALLY needed them to. I can't explain it, but I know I will either be carrying their casket or they will be carrying mine (it just depends on who goes first). It provides me with a level of groundedness that is unmistakable and unmatchable. We've had a lot of history together and a few fun adventures, but now–a-days, the adventures are more along the lines of dealing with painful crap that life throws at us. One guy's wife was recently diagnosed with MS, another guy's 6 year-old was sexually molested. Another guy is going through a nasty divorce where his kids are taking a physical and emotional beating. How valuable is a go-to guy in these scenarios? Priceless.*

*–John*

## FOURTEEN

# Beating the Mountain

*"There are some mountains that take longer to move out the way than others. It's normal at times to feel like the obstruction to your vision, the threat to your hopes and dreams, and the obstacle to your forward movement is going to prevail. However hold fast to your confidence. Speak with boldness and assurance without backing down that you will overcome. You're teaching your mountain how to respect and obey you."*

Dr. Mark Chironna April 4$^{th}$, 2012 facebook post

I've always been a firm believer in just taking that first step. Sitting in a parked car has never worked for me. It just doesn't seem to go anywhere until it gets turned on and starts moving. Does it feel like you are sitting in a parked car? Going anywhere? Those first steps, turning your car on and moving it forward, it's what the Go-To Guys life is all about. No doubt there are plenty of times we are just sitting there feeling stuck on our ledge, but like we talked about before, as men we have to learn how to keep pushing forward. Life is a journey but we must understand our journey as men and embrace the vision God has for our lives as we successfully drive, climb, walk or run the high mountain roads we are conquering. However, we must be moving. In our journeys there is an ascent that requires actually moving and there is a descent off that newly conquered mountain. I believe many men decide to stay in their parked car for fear of failure or fear of not climbing their mountain. The journey encompasses all of it, the successes and the bailing. I have seen some mighty men in my life and they have had bad days, feel they are in a cave, seem to be wandering some desert, but they all have one thing in common; the ability to muster the confidence to trust the vision placed in their hearts and move forward.

It has always fascinated me; those last few steps on Mt. Everest. Even more so, is the debate about whether George Mallory and Sandy Irvine were the first to climb Everest by the Northeast Ridge in 1924. They were last seen by teammate Noel Odell who watched them and described in a dispatch:

> "There was but one explanation. It was Mallory and his companion moving, as I could see even at that great distance, with considerable alacrity ... The place on the ridge referred to is

*the prominent rock-step at a very short distance from the base of the final pyramid." (Noel Odell, The Mount Everest Dispatches, Alpine Journal, No.229)*

They were never seen again. Twenty-nine years later Edmund Hillary and Tenzing Norgay summited Mt. Everest and returned. George Mallory's body was found in 1999 by an expedition trying to discover their bodies and recover the camera in hopes of solving the mystery. Sandy's body has never been found, and it is believed that he carried the camera. Whatever you believe about this debate one thing struck me as I was reading through extremely calculated debates by noted climbers. "Whichever way you look at it, Hillary and Tenzing were the first people to climb Everest and get down again" (Mark Horrell-sept 12th, 2012 blog markhorrell.com). They were the first guys on and off this mountain. Getting to the summit is only halfway on our journeys. Think about that for a moment. It is widely talked about how climbers get summit fever as they push for the summit of Mt. Everest. They ignore their Sherpa's and some have ended up never coming back due to going for the summit at all costs.

Men are so good at going for it at all costs. For some they lose everything because they have chosen to ignore friends, family, and even the Lord. I want to pursue this thought. What if our vision encompassed having a vision that covered ascending the mountain as well as descending it? That we could have a vision that was bred for success! Interestingly enough, the summit is only halfway. Many men spend their whole lives pushing for the summit but never knowing how to return. Their plan for success entails preparing and conditioning themselves but the focus remains just the summit. What I have seen in the Go-To Guys in my own life is a clear vision for success in conquering the mountain, but also a long-term vision for where they are going. It encompasses the ascent and the descent. As we look at the big picture it gives us wisdom and understanding. It helps foster a successful life built around beating the mountain but also getting home.

Let me be clear here. Many amazing men that I know have spent years of their life understanding the season they are in. It's easy to say, "let's have a long term vision, and all will be well". What I'm saying is that the Go-To Guy can move into an area in his life and feel in a desert, or feel his dreams are lost, but he never loses the resolve to keep moving. There is wisdom in pushing through the tough times. Sometimes though these tough times we all have, at one point or another, are the building blocks to gaining wisdom and understanding for the times in our lives. As we walk through them, we begin to see what God had to bring us through to give us the understanding we need to press on further in our journeys. Beating the mountain requires a mindset that rests in the

peace and trust in our Savior to trust His plan for our lives is perfect.
    Recently I was probing a close friend, a Go-To Guy, about how he viewed vision. Each man has to walk his own journey but what transpired was listening to a man who had to walk through a few years of not knowing his vision, not knowing what was next, he still understood what was in his heart and continued forward. As he did that, it allowed God to prepare him for the things that were falling into place. The vision that comes from understanding the long term outweighs the immediate gratification of the summit. We all want to reach the summit, but would we be willing to have the vision for seeing past the summit? There is always another mountain, a bigger one, a much bigger task. As we conquer the mountains in life, Go-To Guys see the mountain they are on, but look on into the horizon, scouting the next ascent. Vision to beat the mountain requires the ability to allow God to fully have discernment in your life. I don't believe a successful life entails making tons of money, having all the houses and cars, and all the worldly offers. What I believe makes a man successful is the ability to carry a vision for the long term; the life you were destined for.
    There will always be times when we feel our vision is obscured or blurry. When we can't see where we are going. It may be dark or foggy. What I am proposing here is that we strive to push into the Lord

for the vision He has for us. This may come easy for some, it may require years of dry times for others. Whatever your journey may be, we must trust that as we push into our identities and remain in relationship with Him, we can believe that He will be faithful to fulfill our dreams. We must keep Him center. He must remain the center of our lives regardless of the storms.

I am blown away by most Sherpa's up in the Himalayas. These guys pack and haul hundreds of people and all their gear every year up Mt. Everest, helping them conquer the mountain. Some of them are summiting multiple times a year. They are the bedrock of most expeditions. They carry wisdom and a wealth of knowledge for even the most trying times on the mountain. How do we gain the wisdom and understanding they have? We must be on the mountain to gain wisdom and understanding about it. We must be moving up the mountain to learn through our experiences. Go-To Guys are chalk full of experiences that are moving them forward. The vision that comes from pursuing your heart unfolds as we seek after what we thought was impossible, and realize that all things are possible if we trust the vision He has for us. Success comes from peace and rest. Beating the mountain comes from trusting years of day in, day out routine.

As we walk out our vision into the future, one thing I have seen maintained is hope. There are definitely times when I feel all hope is gone, but for some reason I can find a reason to muster up some form of hope to keep me going. We must maintain godly hope as we get excited about the direction we are going to conquer the mountain. Hope is contagious as well. As we hang with other men, we absorb some of their hope for something they are excited for as well as rubbing off on others your hope. Hope encourages, it inspires, and it captivates. We must keep hope close as a core value as we step closer to successfully beating the mountain.

So how do we foster a healthy vision as Go-To Guys?

I believe it entails having clear focus of the ascent, summit, and descent. We must carry a vision that carries us up the mountain and off the mountain. The ascent is about looking at the goal and going after it. As we look forward through binoculars we begin to set goals to accomplish the ascent and summit the mountain. All our preparations and motivations come from seeing far ahead what we want to accomplish. As we push towards it, we grow in excitement and as we accomplish mini goals along our way, we walk out a growing longing in our hearts for our dreams. Have you ever met someone who absolutely loves his or her job or his or her pursuit? It seems they are so happy and fulfilled to be working 60-70 hours a week; it almost seems absurd. How can they be so happy with doing that? It's because they are walking out their path, their heart, and their dreams'.

They are walking the path laid out before them, their destiny. Their vision becomes clear.

As we summit our mountains I believe we gain insight into our accomplishments. It gives us a sense of accomplishment. We begin to look at the achievements and the goals we conquer. We also walk out the times when we have to bail off the mountain. I don't believe the summit necessarily means the top of the mountain. Many men attribute the summit as the top, and in most cases it is the top of some goal. There are times however where we gain insight from our failures and tribulations. The ledges and cruxes we face give us great insight to where God has us and where he is taking us. We cannot get there however without first climbing and moving forward. God will direct our paths (Proverbs 3:6). Through insight we can begin to see God's plan for us. Vision requires us first to go after the ascent and through the summit we gain the wisdom to continue on toward that next summit.

The final piece is the descent because it really is like looking at life from a satellite. You can see everything before you, behind you, and in front of you. You can zoom in and zoom out. Having a vision that also entails the descent and beyond gives us the ability to finish strong. This is a core value for the Go-To Guy. Finishing strong is the ability to have a vision that covers not only your dreams but into the lessons, through the trials, and walking out after the dust settles. Failure typically happens when we have a lack of vision. If we cannot see clearly in front of our path, the Go-To Guy uses this time to press into God's heart in worship. As we align our hearts to His, our vision begins to clarify and the fog lifts. You see, the vision you have in your heart can be obscured by your mind and outside influences, but the heart speaks truth. If we are willing to press into our hearts and clearly hear what the Lord is speaking to us, we begin to understand His vision for us. The crazy part is that God's vision for you always has your dreams and desires in mind. For some reason, we as men believe we can come up with some better idea than God can. Some Go-To Guys I know can tap right in to what God is saying. Others have to go through the ringer and to the depths of despair practically to finally align their hearts with His. The ability to walk out the descent gives the Go-To Guy a vision for the long haul.

Beating the mountain requires us to have a view of the present, a plan for the summit, and wisdom for the descent. I laugh now because when you top out on the first summit on Evolution Traverse, there is a clear view of the j-looking ridgeline in front of you. It's then that you realize you have 8 more summits to accomplish your goal! Perspective comes quick when we have a clear view of what's ahead. As we move into being Go-To Guys, having a vision for what's in our hearts is paramount. Success is measured by the ability to get off the mountain as much as it is getting on the mountain. Getting to the summit is really only halfway in our journey. The vision placed in your heart is important.

> *Don't ask what the world needs. Ask what makes you come alive, and go do it. Because what the world needs is people who have come alive. -Howard Thurman*

Foster a vision for the long term. Begin to press in to what is in your heart. It wasn't placed there by accident! As you begin to walk out a perspective that covers the ascent as well as getting home, you will come alive for all that you were destined for. You will begin to appreciate the moments getting there, you will cherish the moments where insight is abundant, and you will use that vision to keep you pressing toward that goal of finishing strong. So what are you waiting for? Get in your car and get going..........

### GO-TO GUY Response

*He (the Go-To Guy) is a man who is settled in his identity from God the Father. Regardless of his childhood, his sense of being loved and being competent (his ability to come through for others-knowing he has what it takes to be a man) comes from his heavenly father. He doesn't need the world's affirmation- He wants to please God, not man. Since I didn't have a model Father, I've been thankful for the fathers the Lord put in my life to help me be a Father. The greatest Go-To guys in our lives can be our fathers. The greatest privilege a dad has is to show his kids what our heavenly father is like: loving, accepting, encouraging, faithful, strong and patient.*

*—Bill*

## FIFTEEN
# Living our Identity

What amazing adventures have you lived lately? How excited were you to get started on that adventure? If you haven't done something recently, what have you desired to do? Our identities come alive as we pursue our hearts. It could be scrubbing in for surgery as your ministry as a physician, it could be the backpacking trip you have always wanted to do, coming alive could look like going to your child's graduation. You see many men are living FOR the adventure instead of living THE adventure. See the difference? Some men are walking around in an empty shell, walking dead per say. They are walking around doing the zombie life waiting until they can get to weekend, or the hunting trip, or the promotion. They are living FOR the adventure. Men have a choice. We can see everything we do as the adventure, or we can just live for the weekends, hoping for some form of release from the mundane. Yes, I agree that sometimes things are the same, day in and day out. However, the Go-To Guy is living who he is, not who he dreams about.

Society today looks to make everyone equal, place us all on the same field. But we are all different. Your identity is something I could never be. I have asked many Go-To Guys I know if they "know" what they are inside. Most of them quickly will respond that they do not know exactly how life will unfold, but that they know deep inside of them what they are capable of. There is a confidence in their identity. Go-To Guys are comfortable in their skin and nobody can change that. What you see is what you get. How do we live out our identity that represents us and not somebody else?

I'm here to say that you can be you. I want to encourage you as either an old man who has lived a long life or a young Go-To Guy in the making, we all can agree that God made you unique. I would venture to say that a struggle we all have is how to live from who we are. Men are so good at attaching to a false identity, one that isn't your own.

> *"Look at superheroes and the sport crazes. Men look at that and take on a persona not their own. Because at the end of the day what do most men have? A job, a family, responsibilities, boring. We need excitement even if its only in our heads living someone else's identity."*
> *–Robert*

Through the years I have caught myself constantly looking at other men and what they have, or what they do for a job with jealousy. I've even been jealous of my best friend for what he carries. Instead of looking at what they are with jealousy, I have worked tirelessly to see them as amazing men, men who carry so much and instill so much wisdom. By seeing them as who they are, instead of longing for what they have, I changed my perspective of my own identity. Really it was a need to feel accepted and capable as a man. We attach to other identities to fulfill those desires. As I worked to dissociate with those identities I wanted to be, it enabled me to understand who I was and clearly hear from the Lord who I was. We need to be comfortable with who we are. We need to understand that these men look up to us as well. The grass isn't always greener on the other side. As my perspective changed, it allowed me to see my closest friends for who they are in Christ, how he made them. These amazing men are in our lives to inspire and walk through life with us, but just like we grow from their wisdom, they grow from ours. Your identity has value. No one else is you. Your identity is yours. I'm just excited because now I can see these men I look up to as men who are walking on this adventure as well. I feel so often we see them on a pedestal. Instead, we should praise God we have these amazing guys in our lives. As we recognize their value, we cherish their godly wisdom. I feel shedding the false identities you have made agreements with is paramount to being free in who you are. If you have areas where you have attached to identities that are not your own, take a moment and lay those at the cross. Ask God to bring you a fresh perspective of your identity and value.

I always have imagined God up in heaven cheering us on as we walk out the destiny He has for our life. He is our biggest fan. Can you imagine God in a sports uniform watching on His massive TV, your life as it unfolds in HD! When you score, He jumps off the couch and screams with praise!! The whole couch is filled with angels and the Lord, probably some wings all stuffed in there, eating some chips. Each goal, or milestone is celebrated. Even in the tough times, everyone is bummed, but they believe in their team, you. You have value. God designed you to be free in who you are.

Living your identity requires a clear understanding of who you are. It requires everything you are to accomplish all He has planned for you. Go-To Guys have this uncanny ability to use their identity to get them excited and motivated for all they are going after in life. Not everything is perfect. But one thing remains true, they are walking out the person they are. So who are you? Take a good look at you. Who are you? When you put your favorite song on, or do something you love, what does it do in your heart? What comes up when you get excited for something close to your heart? Like we talked about before, cultivating a lifestyle that enables you to stay in your sweet spot is what starts us down that road to living our identity. So what makes you come alive? Write down on the side of this page what makes you come alive. Now think for a moment how your identity fits into what makes you come alive.

We have to recognize what drives us and why. For instance, one thing that makes me come alive is running on a small winding trail high in the mountains. What does it show about my identity? I love adventure, being in the middle of nowhere, and can literally feel my reservoir fill up. Part of me needs the adventure and mystique of the mountains. I love pushing myself to the limits. It's my sweet spot. It's what makes me come alive. As we look at what makes us come alive it causes us to see our true selves. The Go-To Guy lives from his identity because he knows through his own life who he is. His life becomes more and more a likeness of what he is supposed to be. This is where I have seen many men look at what makes them come alive and wonder why they aren't doing any of those things! Like we talked about before, we can sometimes get off track or lose our dreams, feel lost. We then connect with other identities, not necessarily our own, only to walk those out. What I'm excited about is men taking back their identities. I want to see men walk out who they are. I have had many opportunities in this life but if I didn't do what was in my heart, it wouldn't be me. The Go-To Guy cannot be duplicated. He inspires and captivates, but he also gets inspired and captivated by others around him that push him. I'm talking about a movement of men here that would not be satisfied with pursuing something not their own. Don't get me wrong, it is very healthy to attach or believe in someone else's vision or business plan, but who you are should not be dictated by that vision or plan. As we align ourselves to someone else's vision we are agreeing with the vision. Our identity does not get changed however. I have seen many times where men will align to a vision only to take on the vision and lose sight of their identity. Instead of aligning to the vision and bringing along their identity, they attach to other identities, and the vision now that they aligned with doesn't work.

The big picture here is that we live and cultivate a culture around us that pushes us deeper into who we are. We can't change who we work with, or the lady in the checkout line who is losing it, but we can surround ourselves with what makes us come alive. We can take steps to cultivate a lifestyle that uses our strengths and weaknesses (your identity) to live THE adventure, not FOR the adventure. It's always good to have goals and look ahead, anticipating the next step, but Go-To Guys have such a desire to live out who they are that they will do anything they can to get there. They are sold out to the vision in their heart. If we are aligned with God's heart then we are sold out to the vision placed in our hearts by Him. What I'm captivated by is how so many men feel

## LIVING OUR IDENTITY

stuck, or are stuck in their current circumstances. How do we as men get out of the zombie life and into an abundant life filled with our dreams and vision? I believe the answer lies in being sold out. Men are amazing at being completely sold out for their futbol team, NFL team, or idea. Once we get an idea that we attach to, there is usually no stopping us in our complete belief of that idea. Growing up here in Idaho as a kid it usually revolved around which truck was better, Chevy or Ford? There were endless outings into the mountains to see which truck could get stuck the worst and get out of it. I'm pretty sure the battle rages to this day. I can remember some heated arguments about which truck is better. It's amazing what men will say to defend something that actually has no real bearing on their life whatsoever! My point here is that we must be sold out with passion for the Lord. Change happens when we align our minds, body, and soul to Him. As a new worship leader at a church, I had a man come up and explain to me that he wasn't going to raise his hands in worship! He felt he wasn't open enough to do it, and in his mind it wasn't going to happen. Years later in a worship set I watched that man open up his arms and fall to his knees in worship. For him, he was coming alive. We must be willing to truly believe as men we were meant to worship, draw near to His word, and be sold out! There will be a time when your identity will impact those around you. Our wives need us to lead them with godly wisdom, willing to drop everything to pray through something together. Our kids need us to be firm anchors for them when the storm gets rough. We come alive and our identities come forth as we push deeper into Him. Success in living out your identity comes when we are willing to allow God to blow wind through our sails again. We cannot be satisfied to sit in our boat with no sails. Don't be the man in a shell getting through life. Risk it all to pull your sails up and begin to take your boat further into your adventure. Look at the things you wrote down. Look at how your identity is wrapped up in what you wrote. You coming alive depends on the choice you have to step into your list. The great thing is that no matter where you are in your adventure, you can always go after more. What's it going take for you to change?

## GO-TO GUY Response

*"I see lots of Bible characters as the "Go-to Guys" with, of course, Jesus being the best. If you needed any kind of healing, just cry-out to Him and He always healed. If you wanted to walk as he walked, give up everything and follow Him. He had the best answer to every problem presented to Him. Another "Go-to Guy" was David. The nation of Israel could go to him to deliver them from their enemies. David's "mighty men" always went to him with their problems and he helped."*

*-Justin*

## SIXTEEN
# The Journey Home

One thing about the Go-To Guy is this: they are on the road less travelled. My hope with this book was never to give a road map or some step-by-step guide to becoming a Go-To Guy. My hope has been to inspire you, motivate you, and keep you moving. My prayer has been that you will see all that you are in Christ. That you will rise up to be the man that God destined in you. My vision is to see a movement of men that are willing to show the world what it means to be a Go-To Guy. Men who are captivated by their dreams and not afraid to risk it all in the pursuit of what the Lord has placed on their hearts. To go after all they want to accomplish in this life. To live a life dreaming big, taking risks, walking in their identities. Men who emulate confidence, cultivate honor and wisdom, and have tender hearts. For some of you, you already know the road less travelled well. For others of you, the trip may just be getting started. But I still haven't found what I'm looking for…

I am an unabashed U2 fan. At my funeral they will play, "Bad", "Where The Streets Have No

Name", and "I Still Haven't Found What I'm Looking for." In that order. I stare at the tag of The North Face clothes in stores with a passion that is indescribable. Never Stop Exploring. I have a passion deep inside me to go after everything in this life. I will never stop exploring. I wake up every morning right now to look over and see my baby girl with her hand held high, trying to touch her toes, and staring in complete wonder in how her little hand moves. I can't wait to show her what's outside that crib. I can't wait to shoulder her and take her to the tops of the mountains. Her smile, just like her beautiful mom, melts me. I believe Christ calls us to be childlike but I also believe He wants to shoulder us and take us everywhere He created. We must position ourselves to be sons, comfortable in who we are, understanding our inheritance. My baby girl barely knows me, but she recognizes my voice and guitar sound from when I played to her through the womb. She feels safe with mommy and daddy, and smiles at us with the most amazing eyes you ever saw! I'm a proud papa. Not for anything I accomplished, but for what God created through my wife and I. As Go-To Guys we have to be willing to impact the world around us. It's our calling. We have to recognize our blessings. The calling is big. It's a challenge. A challenge only worthy of a Go-To Guy. Are you willing to see the calling on your life and respond to the adventure you are being called to?

I can't live out your life for you. I can only show you what I have seen in my own life and those around me. Besides, I'm just going point you back heavenward. Hopefully you have seen in the previous pages that Christ is the ultimate Go-To Guy! Keeping our identity in Him truly does make us more like Him and aligns our heart to His. As we do this we are learning and growing from the ultimate Go-To Guy. My point with our conversation here is to have just that. A conversation. I'm not your teacher. I'm not your pastor. I'm just another guy living what I believe God placed in my heart. My hope is that I can inspire you to live from the deepest place you know, your heart.

One of my favorite things to do before an outdoor adventure is lay out all my adventure gear and sort through my racks of climbing gear, and assorted mountain stuff. It's almost as exciting to me as actually being at the crags. The buildup inspires me. It causes me to dream big. It makes me want to take big risks for my heart. There is purpose in risk. We must as men pursue adventure, whatever it looks like for you. Let's, as men, be transparent, authentic to the core, original. As we push into what it means to be Go-To Guys let's seek after our identities in Christ. Let's live out our identities to our destinies. As we do this, it will naturally cause us to position ourselves to hear what He is saying to us. It's funny too how my body will know that I'm getting ready for a climbing trip and I feel myself get excited to condition myself for the adventure. We must continually position and align our hearts to His just like we would for an earthly adventure. As we prepare for the approach, we condition ourselves to live in freedom. Free to dream. Free to be authentic. Free to be you in your own skin. Free to know who you are and who you are not.

Let's establish and maintain a basecamp through life that protects, and promotes rest. A place to re-energize and refocus your life. Maintain your basecamp as a stepping off point for your destiny. Have an unfaltering attitude that directs your altitude. Seek to have an attitude like that of Caleb, with a vision of the Promised Land to the end. An attitude that overcomes. As we feel ourselves getting off route, learn to recognize the red flags and push to shift into being vulnerable and teachable. We must give God authority in our lives amidst the trials and being off route. Here in Idaho, if you walked into The Home Depot and rounded up all the guys in the store, then asked them to empty their pockets, it would astound you. You would probably feel like you could take down a small country and build a city at the same time. Why? Because most would have Leatherman's, some would have concealed guns, others would have knives, many would reveal cash, keys to large trucks, assortments of clothing, and I'm sure much more. My point is that we have to use the tools we garner from life and what we already have. Our integrity and making choices rooted in wisdom will keep us on the direct route in life. Sometimes we have to be the multifaceted guy. Sometimes we have to use all our tools and weapons at once. Other times we have just the right tool for the right time. Being a Go-to guy requires your utmost dedication and integrity. Let's be men like Joshua and Caleb standing there alone among the crowd. Your critical moments will define you, but they will be a backbone of strength and integrity if you allow the Lord to use them in your life.

When we get to that place where we have to stop and listen, reflect on the Lord, then do it. Position your heart and mind with anticipation for the download. Use your time to praise Him and draw near. Your ledge will take on a totally different look as you change your perspective of it to God's. Like Joshua, we must stay strong and courageous through our cruxes and ledges. Let's be men who learn to recognize the cruxes and know that we are being equipped through our circumstances.

I have always respected snipers. Not for potentially what they are called to do, but for the training and dedication that it takes to make a very long accurate shot amidst seriously stressful wartime scenarios. By allowing God to overcome us with His word and spirit, we can make decisions in trials that reflect God's heart. We can decipher with discernment like snipers do in stressful moments. We must learn to trust God, not the negative outside influences constantly hitting us to foster positive defeat. Let's seek an attitude that encourages based on hope, trust, and belief. Positive defeat defines your identity ultimately driving you to become what you believe.

One area I have been pushing into recently is having a lifelong vision. The Go-To Guy pushes for the vision in their hearts using their confidence to trust the vision. I believe to be successful as men in beating the mountain there has to be a vision for the ascent of a mountain as well as the descent. It has to be a long-term devotion to the calling on your life and to trust it will happen. Our callings can change as we begin to shift our minds from thinking what we believe it should be to what God has for us. As we align to his vision it causes us to see clearly His plan for our lives as we serve and walk out this amazing adventure.

My heart for you going forward is that you live from your sweet spot. The world really does need you coming fully alive. Taking back your identity and walking it out is what I truly want for you. If you already are then awesome! I love to see men sold out to the vision in their hearts. I believe that for you. Don't be afraid to ask God for that vision either. We must be willing to have a sold out relationship in Christ to accomplish all He has for us. What you bring to the table truly is amazing and I look forward to watching you position and cultivating a life and vision that accomplishes the mission God has for you. I pray you find your sweet spot that you can get filled from it as well as have your reservoir spilling out to others. I look forward to finding you on some mountain, and look forward to meeting you. This world is full of amazing men and I'm excited for what God is going to do in you and through you to impact the kingdom and this world. The road less travelled. Invite it, live it, share it.

I want to leave you with this. Through this project many mighty men around this world have contributed their thoughts and insights into what makes up the Go-To Guy. I challenge you to go back, re-read chapters, let it all sink in. Ask the Holy Spirit to come into your life and show you where you can grow, and where you can inspire others. Over the past year I have been going back and reading what these men have shared with me. It is an honor and an inspiration to walk and breathe the same air as these men. They are godly men that are walking out their day to day, not as perfect men, but men willing to listen, willing to be challenged; men wholly committed to the Lord. I trust your journey will be the same. I look forward to hearing what trials and challenges come your way and the men who encouraged you. Most of all I look forward to the man God is making you into and the fulfillment of the destiny and calling he has on your life. What I have learned most from this is that God is continually working in us and if we let Him, He will open up to us more than we ever imagined or could dream! I pray this book inspires you as it has me, and draws you deeper into your own relationships with men you inspire! I look forward to having a Go-To Guy reunion in heaven where we can all get together and share what it meant to have and be the The Go-To Guys............

*Billy*

# Going Forward

**Chapter 1**
- Take a moment and gather the dreams you have. Ask God if there is anything holding you back from your dreams.
- Are you willing to lay down your dreams, longings, and desires for the Lord?
- Going forward invite the Holy Spirit into your dreams, longings, and desires. Invite Him to show you what he has for those deep seeded dreams in your heart.

**Chapter 2**
- Do you have a guy in your life you can get wisdom and encouragement from? Name him here

  _____

- Without sugar coating it, ask your buddy that you named if you are authentic. Ask him if there are areas in your life that he sees are holding you back from being the true you.
- Now ask him to pray with you about those areas, and ask the Lord to remove any area that may be holding back the light from shining through the real you.

**Chapter 3**
- Is your heart positioned to hear God? As you learn how God speaks to you, learn to remove yourself to places or activities that invite your spirit to hear or listen (could be hiking, music, solitude). Decide to spend time once a week there.
- When you get there, ask God to download to you your identity. Refuse to give up asking. Say, "Lord I want to posture myself under You as a son. God, what is my identity in you?" Take time to listen.

### Chapter 4
- Are there areas or struggles in your life you need to condition? What are they? Hint - usually there are struggles we have that cover up bigger heart issues.
- Now think about one of those struggles you highlighted and ask the Lord waht the heart issue of that struggle is. Now go back and do the 1-2-3 skidoo tool again. Nail it to the cross. Remember the words given to you at the end of the tool. These words are Gods promises to you.

### Chapter 5
- What does your basecamp look like?
- Do you have any red flags? Things that are tearing you down, exhausting your resources.
- Choose to break agreements with those red flags. Using discernment, ask the Holy Spirit to highlight waht is breaking you down. "Lord what is breaking me down?" Now ask Him for more of His presence in that area. Ask him for tools to break free.

### Chapter 6
- Are there areas in your life where you act like the ten spies?
- Is your attitude helping you or hurting you?
- Can your attitude change your life?

### Chapter 7
- Do you have something you need to come clean about?
- Share it with your go-to guy.
- Ask the Lord for renewed direction as you overcome the issue.

### Chapter 8
- What are you doing in your life now to stay on the direct route (on course)? When was the last time you accepted hard words from a close friend? Were you able to listen and accept them?
- Choose one thing in your life to work on this week that has been a struggle. Read Proverbs 2:1-11 and apply it to your struggle.

**Chapter 9**
- What agreements have you made with the critical moment you thought of? Did you make a good choice? In your moment of choice (the temptation, the critical moment), why did you make the choice you did? What was driving that decision? Ask God to bring wisdom and understanding to that heart issue.

**Chapter 10**
- What feelings do you have about the ledge you may be stuck on right now?
- Name the good things in the situation and speak them out loud...basically put all feeling aside of how negative the situation is and choose to see the good.
- Are you using your time on your ledge to listen, reflect, and draw near to Him? If not, refocus your eyes on Him. Ask the Holy Spirit to reveal to you what He is speaking while you are on your ledge. Chances are, He's ready to move you off your ledge, but the question remains: Are you?

**Chapter 11**
- Do you struggle with striving in your life? Now go ask your wife, best friend, mom or dad, or someone you trust if they see you striving in your choices and decisions. Listen to what they say and compare it to your own thoughts.
- What do you think is keeping you from pushing past your crux?
- How are you protecting how you make decisions in your life? How do you respond in the face of opposition? What steps can you take to move past your crux?

**Chapter 12**
- How are you choosing to have control over your trial right now?
- Are you waiting on the Lord in your trial or hastily trying to come up with an answer?

- Ask the Lord to overcome your heart. Now declare over your life that because of the cross, you are an overcomer.

**Chapter 13**
- How are you choosing to positively see your circumstance?
- Think of a negative circumstance that recently happened to you. Now speak positive words over that circumstance.
- Say, "I'd rather lose with God, than win without Him." Make a choice to say this every time a negative area in your life arises.

**Chapter 14**
- Is your heart aligned to His? Are there outside influences or areas in your mind obscuring your view?
- Are you fostering a vision for the long term?
- Think about the ascent, summit, and descent as it applies to your journey. Are you walking that out or are there areas to work on?

**Chapter 15**
- Are you living FOR the adventure or THE adventure?
- Are you aligned with someone else's vision?
- Looking at what you wrote down as waht makes you come alive, what does that speak to you about your identity?

**Chapter 16**
- What are you willing to change in your life right now after you walk away from this book?
- What is the calling on your life?
- Are you giving God authority in your life?

www.ingramcontent.com/pod-product-compliance
Lightning Source LLC
LaVergne TN
LVHW051518070426
835507LV00023B/3177